GOD AND MAN UNLIMITED

AF322768

MEL REES

Divine Power Combined With Human Effort
Illustrated in the Management of Life

"There is no limit to the usefulness of one who, by putting self aside, makes room for the working of the Holy Spirit upon his heart, and lives a life wholly consecrated to God."
—*The Desire of Ages,* pp. 250, 251.

Review and Herald Publishing Association
Washington, D.C. 20012

Editor: Raymond H. Woolsey
Design: Howard Bullard

Library of Congress Catalog No. 82-5380
ISBN 0-8280-0159-6
Printed in U.S.A.

This book was originally prepared as a syllabus presented in a course of study at Andrews University, Berrien Springs, Michigan.

Contents

1

STEWARDSHIP—THE MANAGEMENT OF LIFE

Stewardship is the responsibility and accountability that every created being has to God.

The word *steward,* as it applies to every created being, is not generally understood, and the term *stewardship* is usually misunderstood. This fact was illustrated by a theological student who frankly observed, "When the professor said we were going to have four class periods on the subject of stewardship, I thought he was really scraping the bottom of the barrel!"

This attitude is not limited to a few people or a particular location. Most churchgoers associate stewardship with the giving of money, and the parting with one's money in most instances appears to be a painful experience; therefore, the word does not have a pleasant meaning to them. Absenteeism from the worship hour can rise markedly if this sermon subject is announced in advance.

A False Concept

This false concept of stewardship is one reason why many people realize no real satisfaction from their lives. In the desire for worldly things, their perspective is limited;

their entire lives are confined to an existence that has a beginning and an ending. People working solely for these things are going down a dead-end street with no lasting reward for all their labor. Solomon asked, "What profit hath he that hath laboured for the wind?" (Eccl. 5:16).

It is unfortunate that this subject should create an adverse reaction in the minds of many people. But this could be due to the fact that the bulk of the preaching, teaching, and writing on the subject is usually in connection with finance. This gives it a wrong connotation. The giving of money might be an evidence of good stewardship in the handling of entrusted means, but stewardship is not a synonym for money. When it was divinely ordained, there wasn't any money—or any churches, schools, or mission programs. Neither can stewardship be considered a program, a canvass, or a procedure.

It seems strange that in church usage the term should generally be thought of in connection with finance, when in everyday parlance it is always used in association with its real meaning. The word *steward* (with some exceptions) is not as common as the words *foreman, superintendent,* or *supervisor.* Possibly the term *manager* is better understood and more often used as a synonym for steward.

Many times the individuals holding these positions are not responsible for money at all. There are times when finance is their sole responsibility; at other times it is only part of their trust. In each case, however, these persons are responsible for the goods of another person and accountable for its wise and honest management. These persons are stewards, or managers, and their responsibility is stewardship, or management.

The degree of accountability varies with the size and extent of the trust. The fact that they have been entrusted with the possessions belonging to another person proves that this is a position of dignity.

It is essential that each person clearly understands his relation to God, and the lofty plans that God has for him. If he does not accept this concept, then he is little better off than an ant that goes through life rearing its young and trying to store up enough food during the summer months to last through a hard winter. If all there is to living is a day-to-day existence with no life beyond this world, the wonder is that there are so few suicides.

Stewardship Defined

What is a steward? What is stewardship? The dictionary defines a steward as "one who manages the property of another." Stewardship is "the position, duties, and responsibilities of a steward." Stewardship, then, is management. A steward is a manager.

To the Christian manager, this responsibility should be even more relevant, for he is managing the possessions of the Owner of the universe. Only in the framework of this concept does his life have any meaning or direction. An acceptance of this responsibility will permit him to follow a divinely planned blueprint. It will allow him to expand every talent, every capacity. Think of the magnitude of this role!

A steward identifies himself with his master. His master's interests become his. He has accepted the responsibilities of a steward and he must act in the master's stead, doing as the master would do if he were presiding over his own goods. The position is one of dignity, in that his master trusts him. . . . Every Christian is a steward of God, entrusted with His goods.—*That I may Know Him,* p. 220.

It is possible that the average professing Christian does not really understand the meaning of life management according to God's plan because he considers himself an owner rather than a manager. One factor contributing to this attitude may be that most of the appeals made for church financial support approach the member not as a manager but as an owner. The usual request is for *his* time, *his* talents, *his* means, rather than presenting these needs as an opportunity to use that with which he has been entrusted. Often he is praised for *his* service, *his* liberality.

This owner attitude is unfortunate, because every person becomes one of God's managers at birth and remains one as long as he lives. He may be a good manager or a bad one, but he is always a manager—never an owner. Even his life is not his own; it belongs to God, first by creation, and then by redemption. A person who makes no profession is just as much a manager of God's goods as are those who do, for he has also been entrusted with time, talent, and means for which he is responsible and will be held accountable. "So then every one of us shall give account of himself to God" (Rom. 14:12).

Why Talk About Money?

In its truest sense Christian management refers to the relationship that exists between a person and God. Why, then, are money and the material things of life stressed when considering this subject? Are money and material things more important? Jesus said they were not. He taught that one could not serve God and mammon. But He also taught that one could serve God *with* mammon.

In relationship to importance, the management of time is more important than any other talent. "Of no talent He has given will He require a more strict account than of our time."—*Christ's Object Lessons*, p. 342.

Why, then, do the people who devote their lives to teaching this vital subject spend so much time with the material aspects of life?

It is because the world has become so money-oriented. Success, failure, happiness, and discontent are usually associated with the possession or lack of money and material possessions. However, there are three primary reasons why a frank discussion of the material aspects of life is considered important when discussing a person's responsibility and accountability to God.

Focal Point of Selfishness

Money appears to be the focal point of nearly all selfishness. Possibly this is because it is associated with the gratification of selfish desires. It also represents security, and this becomes the life goal of nearly everyone just as soon as he is old enough to recognize that food, clothing, and shelter are essential to life. But Jesus cautioned His followers not to fall into error of seeking for these things. "For after all these things do the Gentiles seek" (Matt. 6:32).

Selfishness is at the root of every other sin. The most logical point to begin its eradication would appear to be at its source. Every Christian must be led to see that self-seeking is contrary to Christian principles. He must realize that money is of no lasting value except as it is used to further spiritual ends. He must understand that security can never be found in the perishable things of this world, no matter how essential they may appear to be. These are all subject to sudden and unpredictable loss. The only true security lies in a simple, childlike trust and dependence upon God. Therefore, the relationship that material things bear to Christianity must be clearly delineated.

Money Represents Life

Money is a visible representation of the actual expenditure of life itself. Someone has said that money is life done up in a convenient package for handling, storage, and use.

The early American author and naturalist Henry David Thoreau observed that people do not ride on the trains—the trains ride on them! To his amazed and somewhat skeptical neighbors he explained that the ties and rails on which the train moves represent a portion of the lives of the men who laid them. Therefore, the train actually travels on the lives of these men.

This also applies to the Christian. When he gives a gift of money to God, he is really giving a portion of his very life—that portion he used in making the money. In this way a person who may never have had the opportunity to go as a missionary can, through his gifts, send a portion of his life to some foreign field.

Call to Reform

God, through the prophet Malachi, called for a reform among His people. "Return unto me, and I will return unto you" (Mal. 3:7). When the people inquired wherein they should return, God referred to a specific point on which they were deficient. They had been robbing Him by withholding their tithes and offerings. God pointed to this as the diseased root to all their problems, for it was a clear evidence of the selfishness in their hearts. This selfishness was infecting every part of their lives.

In the church today, when unfaithfulness in tithing is so evident and when offerings show an alarming percentage-of-income decline, surely the message that God sent to the church prior to Christ's first coming must be the message to His church waiting for His return.

For these reasons, money and material possessions are considered of sufficient importance to discuss specifically when considering the broad subject of mankind's manager relationship to God. Frankly, this is regrettable, for it would be far more pleasant to spend this time studying more deeply into the beautiful plans God has for those who recognize this intimate partnership. Unquestionably, Jesus would rather have spent more time talking about His Father's love and of the wonderful place He was going to prepare, but somehow, in His day as in ours, money always seemed to get in the way.

The Need for Reform

There is need for a genuine reform in the church today. The last warning message, which should be going forward with jet speed, is in many areas slowed to a walk because of the selfishness of God's people. There must be a heart reformation. The work will not succeed without the power of the Holy Spirit, but before this can happen selfishness in all its forms must be banished. "God cannot pour out His spirit when selfishness and self-indulgence are so manifest."—*Counsels on Stewardship,* p. 52.

The Results of Reform

From these and a host of other messages that have been sent to the remnant church, it can be seen how vital it is that every professing Christian thoroughly understands and puts into practice the true principles of life management. Compliance with these will prepare the way for the Lord's soon return. The evidence will be seen in many ways:

First, God will be able to pour out His Spirit without measure and the gospel can go to every corner of the earth. The Holy Spirit will open hearts to receive divine rays of light. It will make the truth impressive and convince souls of the need of a Saviour, and will supply the power essential to conversion.

> When all are faithful in giving back to God His own in tithes and offerings, the way will be opened for the world to hear the message for this time.—*Testimonies,* vol. 6, p. 450.

Second, unselfishness will permit the church to move forward in unity, marching as an army with banners, armed with God's Spirit, impelled and aided by divine power. The world will then witness a force not seen since apostolic times.

Third, an acceptance of the owner-manager principle will be seen in the unselfish use of time, talent, and means in carrying the gospel message. With the debris of selfishness cleared from the channel, God can pour all the resources of heaven into a final thrust that will culminate in the total eradication of sin. Once more peace will reign over all of God's universe, and His faithful managers of perishable things will become the managers of eternal riches. All the universe is waiting for this union of dedicated human effort and divine power.

2

SATAN'S PLANS EXPOSED

The Sabbath reminds man of God the Creator; the tithe, of His ownership.

One of the devil's most carefully laid and well-executed plans has been to destroy the sovereignty of God. His rebellion in heaven was designed not only to overthrow God's government but also to place himself in a position of power equal to that of God. "I will ascend into heaven," he boasted to himself. "I will exalt my throne above the stars of God: . . . I will ascend above the heights of the clouds; I will be like the most high" (Isa. 14:13, 14).

Two of his most subtle and successful efforts to erase the image of God from the minds of men and women have been in the substitution of a false sabbath and in the adulteration of the tithing principle.

False Sabbath Substituted

By instituting a false sabbath he has almost obliterated man's belief in God as the Creator. This unbelief has resulted in the fantastic, man-made theory of evolution. Mankind, through science so-called, has been willing to accept the most preposterous deductions in order to erase the image of God, the Creator. So well has the devil's plan succeeded that some self-styled Christians have even proposed the theory that God is dead.

The Attack on the Tithe

Another, but not quite so obvious, attack on God has been through a false concept of the tithing principle. By distorting the true principles involved, the devil has nearly eliminated the concept in people's minds of God as the owner of the world. His attacks have been subtle and tireless. In the past, his two most successful methods were conformity and compulsion. Today his attack is centered in creating strange attitudes regarding both the tithes and the offerings.

To really understand why these incorrect opinions are prevalent today, one must study the history of church finance. This will show how and when these concepts were adulterated.

Adam Understood God's Ownership

God impressed upon Adam the fact of His ownership by giving him *only* the dominion over the earth. As a constant reminder, a tree was planted in the midst of his garden home that he was forbidden to touch on penalty of death. After the entrance of sin, God gave men and women another reminder of His ownership—the tithing system and the requirements regarding freewill offerings.

Patriarchs Understood

The Bible clearly shows that the patriarchs understood these requirements. Abraham paid tithes to Melchizedek, "priest of the most high God" (Gen. 14:18). Jacob vowed that he would be faithful in this requirement and asked God to provide for his necessities. He recognized that his daily sustenance was entirely dependent on God, that he was incapable of providing these things for himself. But as one of God's managers, he had every right to request and expect them.

To keep the Owner-manager principle in the minds of the Israelites so that they could have the certainty of God's favor and protection, the divinely-ordained plan of tithes and offerings was brought to their attention. As they faithfully set apart one tenth of their increase and gave freewill offerings to God, they would be constantly reminded of His ownership.

But somehow, as time passed the people gradually began to consider themselves as the owners of the houses and lands that God had given them; they forgot that they were only tenant farmers. As God's managers they were guaranteed fertile soil, freedom from pests, and the right amount of rain at the right time. But when they started considering themselves as owners they released God of His responsibility—and proved themselves to be very poor rainmakers! After a time they lost their dignified position as managers and became slaves, serving a cruel people in a foreign land.

The Swing to Conformity

After their return from captivity, the pendulum swung completely to the side of conformity, but they lost sight of the significance of the requirements that God had given solely for their protection.

The Sabbath became a day of minute exactions, the tithe an oppressive burden. Peter referred to these when He said, "Now therefore why tempt ye God, to put a yoke upon the neck of the disciples, which neither our fathers nor we were able to bear?" (Acts 15:10).

The religious leaders of Peter's day laid down arbitrary rules that were so complicated that no one knew when his obligations were met. The freedom that God had provided in every requirement was buried under stern regulations. The great lessons that He designed these ordinances should teach were completely lost sight of in the sanctimonious rubbish of man's interpretation.

Jesus Sets the Record Straight

Jesus taught that in God's sight motive was more

important than conformity—and reaped the wrath of the policy makers. He explained that love for God was the only basis for doing God's will. Conformity was only the fruitage of this love. He emphasized the spiritual rather than the material aspects of life and taught that material things were important only as they were used to advance the kingdom of God.

He said that a changed heart was the prerequisite for a changed life. He unloosed the chains of oppression with which the enemy had enslaved men and women. He set the record straight, showing that God is a loving Father who looks after His children with tender care.

He made the Sabbath beautiful again by saying that it was made for man and was to be a delight. He placed the tithe back in its true perspective, calling attention to some of the weightier matters of the law—judgment, mercy, and faith. For all the legalism He substituted a divine message of love.

Early Church Follows Right Principles

After Pentecost the believers who had been indoctrinated with these principles faced an unusual situation. Many of them were cut off from their families and incomes and were in dire need of the bare necessities of life. All believed in the imminent return of Jesus.

In order to relieve the suffering of the believers and spread the good news of the gospel, men and women were willing to sacrifice everything they possessed. Their motive was a pure, unselfish love for God and for their fellow men. This unusual situation was met in an unusual way, not practiced in any other great religious center.

Paul continued in the early churches the education that Jesus began. He reemphasized that all giving must be a heart experience. "As he purposeth in his heart," he wrote to the Corinthian believers, "so let him give; not grudgingly, or of necessity" (2 Cor. 9:7).

This was a restatement of God's instruction to Moses in the Old Testament. "Of every man that giveth it willingly with his heart ye shall take my offering" (Ex. 25:2).

For the first three centuries after Christ the church was supported by tithes, freewill offerings, first fruits, and gifts of property—most of which were given from the right motives. The Didache, a Christian manual of the second century, instructed the Christians to give from principle, not because of specific needs. They "first gave their own selves to the Lord, and unto us by the will of God" (2 Cor. 8:5). Paul had taught the believers well.

Heresy Makes Adulteration Possible

Eventually, as heresy came in to adulterate the doctrines of Christ, the great principle of man's responsibility as God's managers was lost sight of in the demands for more and more money to support in idleness those who had tainted these doctrines. The church's rapidly expanding structure became a mammoth fund-raising institution. In its insatiable desire for personal gain, the gospel commission was forgotten and every kind of abuse came into being.

Tithing became first a law of the church, then of the state. Offerings lost their freewill nature in the revenue-producing doctrine of salvation by works; the significance of first fruits was lost in the money-hungry demands of the clergy. The property of deceased members found its way into the hands of unscrupulous priests.

When the church and state united under Constantine, secularization became complete and the original purpose of the tithes and offerings was once more obliterated. For centuries Christendom was not only compelled to follow the dictates of an apostate church but was forced to support it, as well. The devil nearly succeeded in completely blotting from men's minds the eternal truth that God is the owner of all.

With the legal powers to enforce its demands, the hierarchy instituted every form of compulsory support that the evil minds of men could devise in order to satisfy its unquenchable hunger for more and more wealth. As it became top-heavy in administration, its demands for money became its primary objective, materialism its main aim.

Reformation Reverses the Tide

Luther spoke out against the abuses of the church. He taught that salvation is free; it cannot be bought or sold. Countless thousands who had been chained in religious darkness eagerly sought to escape their shackles and reached out toward this first glimmer of the light of freedom. God had allowed sufficient time for Satan to demonstrate to all the universe the evil results of apostasy; now He was about to bring His great truths back into prominence.

Tithes Still Buried in Error

The reformers taught the great principles of New Testament stewardship but failed to put these into practice, accustomed as they were to the traditional methods of church support. England, during the time of Wesley, imposed one of the most rigorous systems of tithing in history. With the power and resources of a state-controlled church, an entire nation was enslaved in a vast, complicated tithe-tax structure. The laws were so complicated it was practically impossible for anyone to really understand them or to fulfill their requirements. As a result there were tithe lawyers and tithe courts.

Men and women suffered martyrs' deaths for refusal to comply with these laws. Others were thrown into prison for failure to pay unbelievably small sums. In order to escape from this and other abuses in the church, dissenters such as the Quakers, Puritans, and Pilgrims left their native lands, their homes, and their livelihood. Suffering extreme hardship, they eventually made their way to the wilderness shores of the New World.

Church Finance in Early American History

The financial needs of the early churches in America were limited for the most part to new buildings, their maintenance, and the support of the minister. Foreign missions were not a factor, and offerings for other than local needs were uncommon.

After their unfortunate experience with the tithing

system in their native lands, it is little wonder that it was rarely mentioned. Tithing, to the people and to the ministry, was something to be avoided. John Smyth, an early American preacher, is reported to have said, "We hold that tithes are either Jewish or Popish." Once more the devilish plan to erase this reminder of God and His ownership from the minds of otherwise honest believers was accomplished. In this land where they could have followed God's instructions without opposition, they once more resorted to the inventions of men.

After having seen the evils resulting from a state-controlled church, it is amazing that many of these churches turned back to compulsory support. Some of them held the view that to have a good government and a pure church, the two must be combined. This church-state combination compelled men by law to support the church. Dissenters were dealt with harshly. Thus many found themselves under the same oppressive system from which they had so recently escaped.

Writing on the subject of compulsory support, Benjamin Franklin once said, "When a religion is good, I conceive it will support itself; and when it does not support itself, and God does not take care to support it so that its professors are obliged to call for help of the civil power, 'tis a sign, I apprehend, of its being a bad one."

People Rebelled—Other Means Sought

Eventually the people rebelled against compulsory support, and other means had to be sought if the church was to survive. Incredibly, one of these methods was an excise tax on rum and wine! Other means included ministers' fees, church fines, and pledges and assessments of flour, corn, lard, tallow, hides, tobacco, and whiskey!

Many large churches were built by funds received from lotteries, and their ministers were paid from pew rent. Fancy fairs, bazaars, and many other forms of amusement and entertainment were employed to secure the funds necessary for their operation. Instead of following God's plan for church finance, they persisted in using methods of their own devising—and never found a satisfactory solution.

Out of the multitude of fund-raising schemes, one of the most successful was the every-member canvass. (See chapter 20.) These were conducted by trained "outside" specialists. Regardless of their success, there must be something lacking in the spiritual life of any church when hired professionals, using high-pressure methods, have to be employed to get the members to give money to their church that they would not otherwise have given.

Results of These Methods

For centuries erroneous ideas regarding the tithes and offerings have poisoned people's minds and are responsible for some of the strange attitudes that are commonplace in the church today. To illustrate:

One day a middle-aged Christian secretary stopped by the door of my office. After wishing me Good morning, she surprised me by saying, "I resent every dime of the tithe I pay, because it keeps me from buying the kind of clothes I would like to wear. I resent every cent of the offerings, too, because it keeps me from going to really nice places to eat."

Somehow the thought had never crossed my mind, as I saw her going quietly and efficiently about her duties each day, that she had an inner longing for fashionable clothes or a desire to dine in some exclusive restaurant.

When I recovered from the initial shock, I replied, "If you really feel that way, then I think you should take your tithe and buy the kind of clothes you want. I also think you should use the money you give in offerings to dine in some really nice places."

It was her turn to be surprised. She hesitated for a moment, a look of utter disbelief on her face, then replied, "How can *you*, of all people, say such a thing! Paying my tithe and offerings is my duty—and I'm going to do it if it kills me!" What a strange attitude from one who seemed so mature and satisfied in her religion. Where had her education into the beauties of God's plan in the tithes and offerings been neglected?

It was in the paneled office of a businessman that I received another shock. He began our conversation by saying, "I pay an honest tithe, but as far as I'm concerned it is just a tax—like income taxes . . . and the offerings—they're taxes too."

Why do these unfortunate attitudes regarding this Christian practice exist in this enlightened age? Could it be because today's professing Christians are the descendants of the people who fled the persecution of a tithe-tax system? Has this warped attitude been inherited from generation to generation?

Results of This Attitude

One has only to look around to see the unhappy results of this erroneous thinking. Churches face a constant struggle to match their incomes with their maintenance costs. Mission programs are restricted for lack of funds. People, considering themselves owners of the goods that they possess, show reluctance in parting with other than token amounts. Many feel themselves generous to a fault when giving amounts far below their potential. People are praised for their philanthropy—God is left out of the picture.

But even more serious than the limiting of church and mission programs is the lack of spirituality within the sacred confines of God's house, which these attitudes have engendered. Funds that should be bringing aid and a knowledge of a risen Saviour to a suffering humanity are selfishly used for self-gratification. The result is a spiritually dead church in a dying world. God has such a simple, workable plan for financing His work here on the earth, but Satan has repeatedly tried to destroy it by inducing men to use methods that actually encourage selfishness rather than counteract it. This has been the devil's carefully executed plan to erase the image of God, the Owner.

3

MAN'S RELATIONSHIP TO GOD

Man was never given the ownership of the world or anything in it —just dominion.

No matter how much of this world's goods a person might think he owns, no matter how many deeds of title he might have, he can never be an owner. His claim to ownership is always subject to forces beyond his control. Fire, flood, tornado, conquest, and even termites can make his claims worthless, because mankind has never been able to completely control the environment.

A claim to ownership may even be refuted by the refusal of his fellows to recognize his claim. Legal maneuvering may nullify it. Our great system of superhighways has forced people to move from homes for which they held valid deeds of ownership. And, even if a person could successfully defend his ownership claims during his lifetime, he would have to relinquish them at death, for they will inevitably fall into other hands.

Solomon recognized the difficulty in trying to perpetuate ownership. He said, "Yea, I hated all my labour which I had taken under the sun: *because I should leave it* unto the man that shall be after me" (Eccl. 2:18).

Man's Relationship to God Established

From the beginning, a person's relationship to God has always been that of a manager, not an owner. This fact was clearly established when God said, "Let us make man in our image, after our likeness: and let them have *dominion* over the fish of the sea, and over the fowl of the air, and over the cattle, and over all the earth" (Gen. 1:26).

This fact must have been impressed on Adam's mind by the tree that God planted in the Garden and forbade him to touch. The penalty was severe enough to show how God regarded ownership. From the record it appears that Adam had no difficulty in naming every animal and flower, but he didn't seem able to manage the orchard! After his transgression, he hid from God. Owners don't have to hide. Then he was evicted from his home—he didn't even own that.

The Example of Israel

Just before God brought Israel into the land of Canaan, He instructed Moses to warn the people regarding their attitude concerning ownership. "Beware that thou forget not the Lord thy God," Moses told the people. "It is he that giveth thee power to get wealth" (Deut. 8:11, 18). He said that just as soon as their flocks and herds multiplied and their silver and gold was multiplied and their stomachs were full, there would be a tendency to forget God. He even told them what would happen to them if they forgot. But they could avoid these dire consequences if they followed the safeguards that God had provided to help them remember.

Each year the men were required to go—first to Shiloh, later to Jerusalem—to worship the Lord. At these feasts they were to present their tithes and offerings. There were other requirements that would keep this Owner-manager relation crystal clear.

On the day after the yearly Passover Sabbath, a sheaf of freshly ripened grain (barley) was waved before the altar of the Lord as an acknowledgment that all was His. No grain was to be harvested until this recognition was made.

On the day of Pentecost two loaves of bread, baked with leaven and wheat flour from the new crops, were presented to God as still another expression of their recognition of His supreme ownership.

In the seventh month came the Feast of Tabernacles. This was a time of rejoicing, for the harvest had been gathered into the granaries. On this occasion the choicest of the orchard, the olive grove, and the vineyard were presented to the Lord.

To further impress on their minds His love and watchcare, God protected their lands during their journeys to these feasts. Every man who could make the journey was required to attend. They left their wives with small children and the old people back on the farm. There wasn't one able-bodied man in all Israel to protect these defenseless people from the marauding bands of the enemies that surrounded them. Their protection required a miracle. God simply took the desire for their lands out of the hearts of the heathen during this period when His instructions were being followed: "For I will cast out the nations before thee, and enlarge thy borders: *neither shall any man desire thy land,* when thou shalt go up to appear before the Lord thy God thrice in the year" (Ex. 34:24).

But somehow as time passed, these people lost sight of God as the owner of the lands that they farmed, and found to their sorrow they couldn't hold them against their enemies. They just couldn't control their environment.

The Owner-Manager Relationship

To really understand the Owner-manager relationship, one must recognize the difference between an owner and a manager. In ownership there are unlimited privileges; that is, an owner may use or dispose of his goods as he desires. The manager has certain restrictions, and a violation of these constitutes the crime of embezzlement. Man-made laws have always imposed severe penalties on perpetrators of this crime, for it is a felony.

One of the best illustrations of this limitation in

management is found in the story of the young Hebrew, Joseph. Through no fault of his own (except perhaps for a bit of talebearing on his brothers, and naiveté in telling the family of some unusual dreams) he found himself a slave to the wealthy and influential Potiphar, the captain of the Egyptian Pharaoh's guard.

Because of his faithfulness to duty, Joseph was finally elevated to a position of almost absolute authority in the Egyptian's household. That Joseph recognized that this authority did not include everything his master possessed is clearly shown by his refusal to enter into a liaison with his mistress, Potiphar's beautiful but adulterous wife: "But he refused, and said unto his master's wife, Behold, my master wotteth not what is with me in the house, and he hath committed all that he hath to my hand; there is none greater in this house than I; *neither hath he kept back any thing from me but thee,* because thou art his wife: how then can I do this great wickedness, and sin against God?" (Gen. 39:8, 9).

Joseph recognized that a violation of the restriction in the management of the property of another constitutes a crime. His faithful adherence to this principle was a great bulwark that protected his moral integrity. On the other hand, when Adam took of the forbidden fruit he became an embezzler and was subject to the penalties for the violation.

The First Sin a Violation of This Principle

The first sin in heaven was also a violation of this Owner-manager relationship. Lucifer, a created being, refused to recognize his relationship to God. Cast out from the courts of glory, he enticed Eve by a delusive argument to forget that she wasn't an owner. Adam, because of his fatal fascination for his lovely wife, willingly violated the only restriction in his manager-relationship to God, and has bequeathed to his descendants the inordinate desire for ownership.

Christianity Based on Same Principle

This eternal principle can be seen in the words of Jesus when He said, "For I came down from heaven, not to do mine own will, but the will of him that sent me" (John 6:38). Paul, self-assured, zealous, wasn't a very good manager (for God) until that fateful day on the road to Damascus when, amazed and bewildered, he cried out, "Lord, what wilt thou have me to do?" (Acts 9:6). This is the question of one who is looking for orders from a superior, not the words of an owner. From that time on to the end of his life he strove to accomplish only one thing—the will of his Master.

The problem of the ages has been that people have embraced the pagan theory of ownership rather than the Christian tenet that every person is a manager of God's goods. A Christian looks for a spiritual relationship with his Maker, not to the possession of material or temporal things. It is heard over and over again in his prayers and in the songs that he sings. Without this belief, he would be wasting a great deal of time and effort that he now spends in religious activities. This hope provides meaning and direction to his life that is not enjoyed by the unbeliever.

Right Attitude Brings Security

As a manager under God, a person can enjoy the freedom of dependence. He can be sure that all his plans are under divine control and direction. He also has the assurance that the daily needs of both him and his family will be supplied.

This is what Jesus was trying so urgently to get folks to see in His Sermon on the Mount. He told them that happiness didn't consist in owning things—this produces only headaches. The more things, the bigger the headache. True happiness includes the knowledge that God will provide all the necessities of life no matter what conditions might exist. He explained it by calling attention to God's watchcare over the birds, the grass, and the flowers.

Perhaps a certain farmer understood it best. Reading his well-worn Bible one day, he saw this great truth of God's ownership. Falling to his knees he prayed, "I'm sorry, God. I thought I owned this farm. Now I see You really own it—I'm just the manager. So I'm going to give it back to You. But I hope You'll forgive me, because we do things a bit strange down here. You see, I'll have to keep my name on the deed; but You and I will both know who *really* owns it!"

Down in the little village his neighbors thought he had been out in the sun too long when he told them that he had given his farm back to the one who owned it—especially when they found out it was God. But, not allowing their jests to disturb him, he explained that this took all the worry from his shoulders. "I just get down on my knees each morning and ask God to show me how He wants His farm run, and that's the way I run it—just as good as I can."

One day a plague of grasshoppers came. They ate their way across his neighbor's farm. When they got to his fence they didn't stop, roll over on their backs, and die; they swept across his farm, too, and consumed every blade of grass. The neighbor could hardly wait to see him.

"I'll bet this changes your mind about God owning your farm," he greeted him.

"Why, not at all," calmly replied the farmer.

"I don't get it," said the neighbor.

"It's simple. God owns the farm and He owns the grasshoppers. If He wants to pasture *His* grasshoppers on *His* farm, it's all right by me!"

Job recognized God's ownership when he told his wife, "The Lord gave, and the Lord hath taken away; blessed be the name of the Lord" (Job 1:21). He could suffer the loss of all the possessions he controlled with calmness because he didn't regard them as his. In reality, what Job lost was his job as manager—temporarily.

Rx for Happiness

And so it is with a person who considers himself God's steward—His manager. He can rest in the assurance that regardless of circumstances he is under the direction and protection of the Owner of the world. He can walk in confidence knowing that his Master has a thousand ways to care for him of which he knows nothing.

Jesus explained it this way: "Come unto me, all ye that labour and are heavy laden, and I will give you rest. Take my yoke upon you, and learn of me; for I am meek and lowly in heart: and ye shall find rest unto your souls. For my yoke is easy, and my burden is light" (Matt. 11:28-30).

Placing trust and confidence in God at all times and under all circumstances will free a person from worry over the uncertainties of life. This can only be experienced when he recognizes that God is the Owner—he is only the manager of the things with which he has been entrusted. This is the position for which he was created.

4

MAN'S TEST IN THE PLAN OF REDEMPTION

God is testing man with perishable things to determine his ability to manage eternal possessions.

The greatest gift that the Creator gave to Adam wasn't the dominion of the world or the beautiful home in Eden; it was the power of choice. Satan had accused God before the universe of being a dictator, One who forced His subjects to obey. When God gave man the power to choose He proved that Satan was a liar. The very fact that he could disobey proves beyond doubt that he had this God-given choice.

God's government is founded on the love principle, and the only service that is acceptable must be the result of this principle. God loved the man whom He had created. He wanted this love returned from choice, not from filial duty or by force.

But there was another reason why God gave man the power to choose. He was given dominion of the world. Management requires decisions. Adam needed the power of choice if he were to carry on his work successfully. Of course, God could have hooked him up to some type of celestial computer, like a robot, and programmed him to do exactly as He wished. But this would not be compatible with the character of God, which is love. Adam was crowned king in Eden. To prove his love and devotion to God, a tree was placed in the midst of Eden and he was warned not to touch it. Just as long as he remained obedient to God's command, he was to have access to the tree of life, which would perpetuate his existence. When Adam disobeyed God he lost the dominion of earth; it passed into the hands of his conqueror.

Race Doomed

His sin brought the inevitable penalty of death upon the whole human race. Except for the mercy of God, they would have passed into oblivion. "Without the grace of Christ every soul would have been bankrupt for eternity."—*Testimonies to Ministers,* p. 166. But God's only Son, Jesus, volunteered to take the sin of mankind upon Himself and to make atonement for the fallen race (see *The SDA Bible Commentary,* vol. 1, p. 1082). Now no one could doubt God's love and mercy. He was vindicated before heaven and the universe, who, we are told, would have been just as happy if He had left mankind to perish *(That I May Know Him,* p. 367).

Christ's Sacrifice Guarantees Choice

The death of Jesus upon the cross does not guarantee any person salvation or eternal life. It only assures him of the *right to choose* eternal life, and makes provision for this choice. He can refuse to accept Christ's atonement for his sins. He can reject God's mercy. But Christ's sacrifice permits every man and woman to stand in the same position as Adam did the day he came from the hand of the Creator—with the freedom to choose. Not one person will ever be able to say that God is unfair, that he must die for something he didn't do. If he dies eternally, it will be by his own choice.

Man to Regain Dominion

The plan of redemption was designed to permit man to regain the dominion that he lost through disobedience.

Much has been written about the paradise that was lost and of the paradise that is to be regained. But what was this paradise? In the minds of many people it was a sort of never-never land of quiet and solitude where there wasn't much going on or much to do. Too often the picture of heaven and the new earth involves some fleecy clouds and white-clothed saints playing endless tunes on their golden harps.

But Adam and Eve were given the management of a vast creation. They had a great deal to keep them interested and occupied. The paradise aspect of their situation was the ideal condition under which they lived and worked.

How can anyone fail to see that the paradise that is to be regained will also be a land of productive activity. "And they shall build houses" certainly denotes action. "And they shall plant vineyards" (Isa. 65:21) should create the lovely pastoral scene of people working. Once more, the paradise aspect will be the ideal condition under which men may live and work.

Everyone Tested

However, before men may enter this glorious land they must be tested to determine if they can be trusted. "We should never forget that we are placed on trial in this world, to determine our fitness for the future life."—*Counsels on Stewardship,* p. 22.

Imagine what would happen if God accidentally allowed selfish folk to enter the pearly gates. Their eyes would fairly bulge from their sockets as they saw the scintillating foundations of the city and the streets of transparent gold. Their only desire would be to dig up as much as they could and hide it before someone else got there. They'd dig holes all over the universe!

God can't afford to take another chance with His beautiful creation, so He is making sure that everyone eligible for citizenship will have passed the required tests down here.

In the light of this reasoning, it is strange that anyone could preach or teach that in order to be saved it is only necessary to believe—that no tests are involved. If this were so, then Adam suffered a terrible injustice, for he was required to pass a test in order to perpetuate his eternal existence.

Jesus referred to this testing period in the story of the rich man whose soul was required of him one fateful night just when he thought he had it made. The same truth was brought to the attention of the early churches: "So then every one of us shall give account of himself to God," Paul wrote to the Romans (Rom. 14:12). "Moreover it is required in stewards, that a man be found faithful," he cautioned the Corinthian believers (1 Cor. 4:2).

Too often this testing portion of the plan of redemption is passed over lightly or is sadly neglected. The idea that a man has no responsibility except to believe appeals to the selfish heart, but it is not an accurate idea.

When the cases of all come in review before God, the question, What did they profess? is never asked, but, What have they done?—*Ibid.*, p. 129.

While faith is the key to acceptable service, faith will always be demonstrated by corresponding works. These works will be the outgrowth of a living relationship to God. Those who enter the pearly portals will have proved themselves efficient and faithful managers of the time, talents, and material things with which they have been entrusted.

Adam Faced Tests

The original tests required of Adam and the tests today are similar because of the points tested. Adam was tested on obedience, recognition of God's ownership, love, and faith. Men are being tested today on these same points. While no tree of knowledge of good and evil is involved, God has specified certain areas in which the same tests apply. These areas are (1) the Sabbath, (2) the tithe, (3) freewill offerings, and (4) the remainder of one's trust. Of course, each of these elements is of immense positive value, but in a sense our relationship to them constitutes a test.

1. *Sabbath*—one-seventh of time. A test of obedience to

    God's commands

2. *Tithe*—one-tenth of increase. A test of recognition of God's ownership
3. *Freewill Offerings*—time, talent, means. A test of love and faith
4. *Management of remainder of trust.* A test of the attitude and direction of life

The Sabbath—A Test of Obedience

God told Adam, "Of the tree of the knowledge of good and evil, thou shalt not eat of it" (Gen. 2:17). God tells us, "Remember the sabbath day, to keep it holy. . . . The *seventh* day is the sabbath of the Lord thy God" (Ex. 20:8-10). God could have designated the first day of the week, the beginning of Creation, as a sort of groundbreaking memorial, as it were. He might have specified the sixth day when He created man—after all, He said the Sabbath was made for man. But He set apart the seventh day as His memorial to a completed creation. The test is simply obedience to an explicit command—a recognition of the existence and creatorship of God.

The Tithe—A Test of Recognition

The tree placed in the garden belonged to God. By refraining from touching it Adam would have shown his recognition of God's ownership. God tells us, "All the tithe of the land, whether of the seed of the land, or of the fruit of the tree, is the Lord's" (Lev. 27:30). When one regards the tithe as belonging to God, he shows his recognition of God's ownership. God has instructed that His share is to be 10 percent—not 9, 6, or 3—exactly 10. It is a case of simple honesty and recognition.

Freewill Offerings—A Test of Love

In the divine arrangements, man is permitted to manage the remaining 90 percent of his income. While this also belongs to God, he is given full control of its use and dispersal. Part he is permitted to return to God in freewill offerings of love and gratitude, part he can use for his daily sustenance, part to increase his stewardship, and part he can save for "rainy day" emergencies.

The test in the freewill offerings of time, talent, and means is love:

> God permits us to show our appreciation of His mercies by self-sacrificing efforts to extend the same to others. This is the only way in which it is possible for us to manifest our gratitude and love to God. He has provided no other.—*Ibid.*, pp. 18, 19.

It is possible to give without loving, but it is impossible to love without giving. "God so loved the world, that he gave" (John 3:16). Implanted in the heart of every individual is this love factor. A man's love for God will be demonstrated conclusively by what he does—not by what he professes. A common expression applies: "Talk is cheap; it's what one does that counts."

Management of Remainder—A Test of Attitude and Direction

One could observe the Sabbath meticulously from sundown to sundown—the first test; one might be so accurate in his tithing that even a heavenly auditor could find no error—the second test; one might be recognized as a very liberal giver—the third test; but in spite of these virtues, he might fail miserably if he did not also consider the importance of his management of the remainder of his time, talents, and material goods—for God is owner of all and we are therefore responsible to Him for the management of the entire life.

What does one do with the remainder of his time after he has kept the Sabbath? This also belongs to God, and as a manager man is accountable—"Six days shalt thou labour" (Ex. 20:9). What about the remainder of his talents after some have been used in the work of the church? What about the balance of his money? God owns all these. They are entrusted to men and women to be used prudently. They are responsible for their total stewardship, and will have to give an account.

How one uses the remainder of his trust will determine

his attitude toward God and His work. It will indicate the direction of his life. Too many Christians consider their obligations to God as having been met after they have devoted a minimum of time and service. The remainder of their lives is devoted to self. They will be sadly disappointed when their accounts are opened for inspection.

The character is revealed, not by occasional good deeds and occasional misdeeds, but by the tendency of the habitual words and acts.—*Steps to Christ,* pp. 57, 58.

Once more, the attitude is of the utmost importance. Is one a manager or an owner? If a person desires to be a faithful manager he will have no difficulty with the tests that God has ordained for "entrance examinations" to the New Earth. He will simply depend fully on the Owner for instruction and direction. This will free him from worry and concern, for in this position he is responsible only for an honest day's labor, or the efficient operation of a business or profession, realizing that at all times he is working for God. The tests will only demonstrate that he is safe to save. His love and devotion to duty will so control his thoughts and actions that it is doubtful that he will recognize these as tests at all, but simply as a joyful fulfillment of his Master's wishes. The only principles that God ever gave His followers were to keep them healthy, happy, and holy.

Every Man Can Choose

This is the testing period and these are some of the major tests. However, one must never lose sight of the fact that if Jesus hadn't come to this world and died on the cross of Calvary, there wouldn't have been any tests. It wouldn't have made any difference what a person might have wished to do—*he wouldn't have had a choice.* But for His sacrifice, there wouldn't have been any eternal reward, no mansions, no homes in the New Earth. This was love in its purest form—the love for an unworthy, unlovely sinner. In view of such a sacrifice, the tests appear entirely too easy. But such is God's love for man. "If you love Me," He invites, "keep My commandments."

5

MAN'S PART IN THE PLAN OF REDEMPTION

If men will become channels through whom Heaven's blessings can flow, God will keep the channels supplied.

Man was the crowning act of Creation. He was perfect in organization, and beautiful in form. His body was heir to no disease, and he was given an endurance that has withstood the ever-increasing weight of disease and defilement for six thousand years.

When he came from the hand of the Creator, every organ, every faculty, was equally developed and harmoniously balanced. He was made for magnificence! He was to be the ruler of this world! Imagine his potential. Every faculty was capable of development, and he had the privilege of face-to-face communion with his Creator. God had such lofty plans for this man who was to be as a son to Him.

It was . . . [God's] purpose that the longer man lived the more fully he should reveal this image—the more fully reflect the glory of the Creator.—*Education*, p. 15.

His mind and thoughts would have been as the mind and thoughts of God.—*The SDA Bible Commentary*, vol. 1, p. 1082.

It was God's purpose to repopulate heaven with the human family, if they would show themselves obedient to His every word.—*Ibid.*

Man Without God

But man failed to pass the test and spoiled God's beautiful plans. Men and women, floundering in the quagmire of their own wisdom, have been so eager to exclude God from the sovereignty of the universe that they have lowered mankind to the level of their own narrow concepts. They have been willing to degrade him and defraud him of the dignity of his origin. Through the theory of evolution they have dragged this noble creature, made by the hand of God, into the mire of some dismal swamp and pictured him crawling out on all fours into the dawn of history. No wonder the apostle Paul exclaimed, "For the wisdom of this world is foolishness with God" (1 Cor. 3:19)!

Consider what sin has done to this noble creature. At his worst we see him lying in a gutter, his vital strength gone, his God-given powers and faculties dwarfed, his senses dulled, his days as a shadow. At his best, without Christ, he is a strutting, egotistical, selfish little creature, elbowing his way through life, always striving for goals beyond him. At his best or worst he is a slave to his environment, a slave to the things he makes. But God gave man dominion over all the earth. He never intended that the being He had created in His own image would ever be a slave to anything.

Man—Key Figure

Man was a key figure in God's plans for the earth in the beginning. He has also a most significant part to play in the plan of redemption as a copartner with God. He is the channel through which the resources of heaven are to flow to the earth. He is to combine his talents with divine power. To a great extent he has also failed in this plan. What a disappointment he must be to the God who made him.

A Parallel

God's church has always had a mission, but there have been times during the history of the world when it has taken on special urgency. One of these was prior to the first coming of the Messiah; another is this present age just before His second appearing. These two periods have a strange, almost frightening, parallel:

1. The Israel of that day was appointed by God to be a depository of truth to the world.

Today, the remnant church is to be an exhibit to the world of God's truth.

2. The church of that day was to prepare the world for the coming of the Messiah.

The remnant church is to prepare the world for His second coming.

3. Possessing spiritual and material blessings, they selfishly appropriated these and God sent them a message of reproof. But He promised, "Return unto me, and I will return unto you" (Mal. 3:7).

The church today is showing the same selfish lethargy and needs the same messages that lead to repentance and reformation.

Malachi was inspired to give this prophecy not only for the instruction of Israel but "for our admonition, upon whom the ends of the world are come" (1 Cor. 10:11).

Very recently I have had direct light from the Lord upon this question, that many Seventh-day Adventists were robbing God in tithes and offerings, and it was plainly revealed to me that Malachi has *stated the case as it really is.—Testimonies to Ministers*, p. 60. (Italics supplied.)

Today, as in the time of Malachi, the Lord is saying to His people, "Return unto me, and I will return unto you." He is asking men and women to pursue with vigor the purpose He has for them in the plan of redemption.

Men to Be Channels

In *Counsels on Stewardship*, Ellen G. White presents one of the most vivid pictures of man's part in the great plan of redemption: "If men will become *channels* through which heaven's blessing can flow to others, the Lord will keep the channel supplied."—Page 36. (Italics supplied.) The world, in its sinful state, is in desperate need of the good news that Jesus has died to save men. There are millions who need the necessities of life, food, clothing, and shelter. In heaven's vast storehouses there is an abundance of everything the world needs. How are these unlimited resources to be transported from heaven to earth?

God has such a simple plan: *"If men will become channels."* All the bounties of heaven are to flow through the hands of His faithful managers. It is easy to visualize a person holding out his hand to God. God fills it—he transfers these blessings to his other hand and distributes to his fellow men. He holds out his hand to God again and again and again. It becomes a continuous flow from heaven to earth—heaven bestowing, man distributing. Long before people thought of assembly-line production God had implemented it in the plan of redemption. The only reason why God's work is not progressing with speed and power as it should is that either men and women have refused to become channels or that the channel has been obstructed by the corrosion of selfishness.

"If men will become channels." This is the human part of the plan.

Human Effort With Divine Power

In everything that pertains to the sustenance of humanity can be seen the divine formula—human effort combined with divine power. A human being prepares the soil and plants the seed, but it is divine power that causes the seed to spring into life. God alone can provide the sunshine and showers for its growth.

But God has given man a most important part. The life in the seed will lie dormant until the human agent places it in the ground. There is fertility in the soil, but it will not be used unless man does his part. So it is in every activity—in the business life and in professional pursuits. Man has a vital part to play, but he will never be successful unless there is a union of the human with the divine.

This is true even for a person who refuses to recognize

his Owner-manager relationship to God. Jesus called attention to this when He said, "For he maketh his sun to rise on the evil and on the good, and sendeth rain on the just and on the unjust" (Matt. 5:45).

This same principle can be seen in the plan of redemption. The human agent is dependent upon divine power in the saving of lost humanity. Man is to sow the gospel seed. God, through His Spirit, makes Himself responsible for the harvest.

When we give ourselves wholly to God and in our work follow His directions, He makes Himself responsible for its accomplishment.—*Christ's Object Lessons*, p. 363.

Note carefully the important role that God's Spirit has in soul winning:

It is the power of the Holy Spirit that gives efficacy to your efforts and your appeals.—*Evangelism*, p. 285.

The Holy Spirit *will open* hearts and minds to receive the rays coming from the source of all light.—*Ibid.*, p. 436.

It is the Holy Spirit that makes the truth impressive.—*Ibid.*, p. 299.

It is the work of the Holy Spirit to convince the soul of its need of Christ.—*Ibid.*, p. 283.

Learning, talent, eloquence, every natural or acquired endowment, may be possessed; but, without the presence of the Spirit of God, no heart will be touched, no sinner won to *Christ.—Testimonies*, vol. 8, p. 21.

No amount of education, no advantages, however great, can make one a channel of light without the cooperation of the Spirit of God. The sowing of the gospel seed will not be a success unless the seed is quickened *into* life by the dew of heaven.—*The Desire of Ages*, p. 672.

The Holy Spirit is vitally important in soul winning, but God also gave to man his role. God could have carried on the entire work without the human agent, but in His wisdom He saw that this would not be for the best interest of the people He wants to save.

God has made men His almoners, copartners with Himself in the great work of advancing His kingdom of the earth; but they may pursue the course pursued by the unfaithful servant, and by so doing lose the most precious privileges ever granted to men. For thousands of years God has worked through human agencies, but at His will He can drop out the selfish, the money-loving, and the covetous. He is not dependent upon our means, and He will not be restricted by the human agent. He can carry on His own work though we act no part in it.—*Counsels on Stewardship,* pp. 198, 199.

Why did God enlist men and women as His copartners in the work of redemption? In order for a person to enjoy the company of heavenly intelligences, it is essential that he have a completely selfless character. A selfish person is never happy on this earth, and he wouldn't be happy in heaven. True happiness is found only in unselfish love and devotion to God.

It has been reported that the famous Dr. Albert Schweitzer, when offered a position of great honor as head of one of the world's leading medical institutions, replied that he had found a place of service ministering to the poor of Africa—this was enough.

Men and women are selfish by nature, and the development of an unselfish character is a difficult task—one that requires diligent, continuous effort. An unselfish character cannot be formed in the acquisition or retention of the blessings that God has bestowed. Only by constantly sharing these blessings can a person develop this prerequisite for entrance into heaven and the New Earth.

Therefore, God made man His partner in the plan of salvation to make it possible for him to develop a character of selflessness. It could be accomplished in no other way.

God planned the system of beneficence, in order that man might become like his Creator, benevolent and unselfish in character, and finally be a partaker with Christ of the eternal, glorious reward.—*Ibid.,* p. 15.

I was standing in front of a Midwestern church one day

with one of the local elders, a professional man. I had just concluded a short series on the great principles of life management. The members of the congregation were planning the expansion of their school. During one of the meetings the principal had explained the benefits that this expansion would bring to Christian education in the area. An architect had displayed and explained the plans.

"I wish," the elder began, "that you would explain these Owner-manager principles in the practical setting of this expansion program."

"Let's suppose," I replied, "that I am the agent for a great philanthropist who lives on the West Coast. My work is to find suitable projects in which to invest his money, things in which he is interested and which will bring returns on the investment.

"When I heard the principal tell of the benefits to the youth that this expansion will bring, I recognized immediately that this was a project in which my employer would be vitally interested. Let me explain that he is very concerned for the youth today and throws the weight of not only his influence but also his wealth behind any project that will guide them into a better way of life.

"It never occurred to me if I would invest some of his means in this project—only how much. I must give him an account of this investment so I must determine how much my employer would invest if he were here handling his own money.

"Now let's stop supposing. You *are* the agent of a great Philanthropist. He doesn't live on the West Coast; He lives in heaven. You know how vitally interested He is in the youth and in Christ-centered education. When you listened to the explanation today and saw the architectural drawings, the thought should never have crossed your mind if you would invest in this project—but how much. How much of your employer's means would He want you to place in this particular project?"

He thought for a few moments, then, raising his head, smiled and said, "My, it surely makes it easy when you talk about giving someone else's money away, doesn't it?"

"Yes, it does," I answered. "But do *you* have any money?"

"I guess not," he decided. "But I thought I did."

"If men will become channels." Once more one must come back to the same, critical question: Am I an owner or a manager?

The answer to this question is the answer to whether a man fulfills his place in the plan of redemption. A man who considers himself an owner may give to many worthy projects, assist the poor, and do other acts of kindness. But in each case he will consider himself as a philanthropist.

On the other hand, a man who considers himself as one of God's managers will also assist his fellows in every way he can—but only as an agent for the Philanthropist. As an agent he becomes a channel through which heaven's blessings can continually flow down to this world. This is his divinely appointed role in the great plan of redemption.

6

THE MEASURE OF A GIFT

A gift to God cannot be measured by its size, but by the degree of sacrifice that it represents.

It is easy to picture Jesus sitting in a boat on the blue waters of Galilee, with people crowding the rocky shore. The buzz of excitement fades away and a hush falls over the multitude as He begins to speak: "Behold, a sower went forth to sow." The small boys playing at the water's edge stop to listen.

Or one can see Him seated on the lush, green grass of a hillside, a little swale and the opposite hillside forming an amphitheater. But a murmur escapes the lips of the seated throng when He says, "Take no thought for your life, what ye shall eat." What a strange statement to make to hungry people.

It isn't difficult to picture Him seated at the festive table in Cana, enjoying in quiet dignity the happy conversation of friends and neighbors. Or the scene at Jacob's well where the woman of Samaria appeals, "Sir, give me this water, that I thirst not, neither come hither to draw."

But it is much more difficult to visualize the story recorded in Mark 12:41: "And Jesus sat over against the treasury, and beheld how the people cast money into the treasury."

It seems so strange that Christ, with such a monumental task and such a brief period in which to accomplish it, would take time out on one day just to watch the people putting their gifts into the treasury.

Even the disciples didn't appear to be too interested. They were probably looking at the great stone pillars and the craftsmanship of the massive doors, or possibly the intricate gold inlays in this building of which they were so proud.

As Jesus watched, a poor widow stopped by the great Temple chest. Looking furtively around, she dropped in two tiny coins and tried to slip away before she was noticed. But she heard Jesus call His disciples to Him and say, "Verily I say unto you, That this poor widow hath cast more in, than all they which have cast into the treasury" (Mark 12:43). Peter, who was probably impressed with the large gifts of the wealthy, as are most folks today, might have said, "Now, wait just a minute!" or something to that effect.

Heaven's Scales Are Different

It is common to hear praise for some person of wealth because of his large donations, but it would be a rare experience to hear the small gift of a poor person acclaimed. Still, this is what Jesus said. Therefore one can reason that the scales that Heaven uses to measure a gift must be entirely different from those used by the world.

Jesus used this experience to teach His disciples the difference between equal giving and equal sacrifice. Somehow Christians have entirely missed this great principle in both their giving and in their evaluation of gifts. They are accustomed to using the "nose count" method, which, simply stated, is to divide the amount of money needed for a given project by the number of members in the group and assign an equal goal for each member, regardless of his financial potential. Then the gifts are measured by each other and the givers are evaluated accordingly. This results in some strange situations that were never intended by God.

I was sitting in a man's house one day discussing a church building program. The two cars in the open garage, the house, and the furniture all gave indication of affluence. My host made this statement: "We wouldn't be having trouble with our building program if everyone had done his part." I asked, "How much is this part?" He answered, "Fifteen hundred dollars."

An hour or so later I was in another home; here the car in the driveway, the house, and the furniture led me to believe that keeping all the bills paid was a constant struggle. The man, a member of the same church as the first person I visited, said, "We wouldn't be having trouble with our building program if everyone had done his part—but I couldn't do mine. I have a boy in college, a girl in the academy, and two youngsters in grade school—I just couldn't make it."

"How much was your part?" I inquired. "Fifteen hundred dollars," he replied. "I was only able to give about six hundred. I feel guilty, but that was the best I could do."

Equal Giving Is Unfair

Isn't it strange how hard people make it for each other when God makes it so easy? This thought crossed my mind one day when I was climbing the gradual step-incline that leads from the marketplace in old Jerusalem to the Damascus Gate.

An old man was making his way up the street with a large box on his back. On top of this box was another, secured by a band around his forehead. He was stooped and moved very slowly. I recognized him as a professional burden bearer. I wondered how heavy the boxes were, so I followed him.

About a block or so beyond the city walls he stopped before a small shop. Two men came out and took the boxes and placed them on the sidewalk. When I saw with what difficulty they handled these boxes I realized how heavy they must be. I recalled the statement made by Jesus. "For they bind heavy burdens and grievous to be borne, and lay them on men's shoulders" (Matt. 23:4).

How easy it is for people who do not wish to carry their proportionate share to bind heavy burdens and lay them on other people's shoulders. "All therefore whatsoever they bid you observe, that observe and do; but do not ye after their works: for they say, and do not" (verse 3).

Jesus said that the poor widow cast in the greater amount, but her gift wouldn't be considered this way where equal giving is practiced.

The Smallest Was the Greatest

One might wonder why the Master said her gift was the greatest when it was so small it could easily have been lost in a corner of the great chest. But He was contrasting Heaven's measure of a gift with the world's evaluation. People are impressed with the amount, but Heaven weighs the degree of sacrifice involved.

In every group there are various levels of ability and potential. This is true in the potential of health, strength, talent, or financial capacity. In this story the poor widow would have been on the bottom level, a wealthy person on the top.

Jesus said that she had given more than any of the others because she had included part of her very living. Did God require this? No, God never asks anyone to give beyond his ability. Then why did she make such a sacrifice? She loved God and His house. She wanted to express this love, but looking into her tiny store she couldn't find enough to adequately fulfill the desire she had in her heart, so she added a part of her very living in order to satisfy this longing for expression.

The Wealthy Could Have Equaled Her Gift

A wealthy person could have equaled her gift—if he had given everything he had plus his next meal. But God would not ordinarily require this unless there was some unusual situation, as was the case of the rich young ruler who wanted to inherit eternal life. In that instance the eradication of selfishness required a total sacrifice.

God has had many faithful managers such as Abraham, Isaac, and Jacob who were responsible for great possessions. It is no sin to possess wealth. The sin is in hoarding wealth or in its selfish use.

Equal Sacrifice Is Fair

God has endowed people with talents of time, ability, and means. He requires a portion of these trusts to be used in His great plan of redemption so that it may accomplish its purpose on the earth. This requirement is founded on the principle of self-denial, not the amount given.

The same principle was set forth in the Old Testament in the instructions given to the Israelites for their freewill offerings. "Every man shall give *as he is able,* according to the blessing of the Lord thy God which he hath given thee" (Deut. 16:17). This placed no burden on anyone. Neither was any person to be subjected to the criticism of another because he had not "done his part" as measured by the standards of the world.

There is only one instance in the Bible where equal giving was required, and that was in the case of an atonement, or a ransom, for the soul. The amount specified was to be exactly a half shekel. "The rich shall not give more, and the poor shall not give less" (Ex. 30:15). In this God clearly taught that men's and women's souls are of equal value, whether rich or poor.

Paul emphasized the principles of equal sacrifice. "Let every one of you lay by him in store, as God hath prospered him" (1 Cor. 16:2). "It is accepted according to that a man hath, and not according to that he hath not" (2 Cor. 8:12). These two references clearly set forth the principle of individual ability.

God's love and justice can be seen in this principle. He never intended that anyone should enter his church reluctantly because he was unable to bring a specified amount. Giving was to be an expression of love and gratitude. Salvation was free to everyone. "Ho, every one that thirsteth, come ye to the waters, and he that hath no money; come ye, buy, and eat; yea, come, buy wine and milk without money and without price" (Isa. 55:1).

The Motive Is the Important Thing

In heaven's balances the size is of no importance. It is the motive and the degree of sacrifice that are the measure of a gift. Man is unable to judge motive; neither can he evaluate the degree of sacrifice that any gift represents. Therefore he must be very careful in his estimation of any gift, regardless of its size. He should remember, "God considers more with how much love we work, than the amount we do."—*That I May Know Him,* p. 167.

7

ACCEPTABLE AND UNACCEPTABLE OFFERINGS

Every gift to God must bear the test of His acceptance.

What motivates a man to give is more important than how much he gives. One wonders if the thought has ever occurred to many professing Christians that God might not accept some of their offerings regardless of how many goals they might reach or the size of their gifts.

Jesus told about some people who had reached some very impressive objectives: "Many will say to me in that day, Lord, Lord, have we not prophesied in thy name? and in thy name have cast out devils? and in thy name done many wonderful works?" (Matt. 7:22). But He said He would profess He never knew them. Something must have been terribly wrong.

Importance of Motive

Paul called attention to the importance of the motive in service to God. "And though I bestow all my goods to feed the poor, and though I give my body to be burned, and have not charity [or love], it profiteth me nothing" (1 Cor. 13:3). Ellen White said God would regard such a person as a *"deluded enthusiast or an ambitious hypocrite"* (*Testimonies,* vol. 5, p. 168).

These references show how important the motivation is in giving to God and His cause. Every offering should be studied to determine if the motive is right, and if it would be acceptable to God.

One of the first two recorded offerings made to God was unacceptable. The offering that Cain brought no doubt represented sweat and hard labor. By today's standards he would probably have been considered a generous man and his offering worthy of praise. But in God's sight it was an abomination, because He knew that it was the gift of a rebellious heart. The motive was wrong.

The gift of Ananias and Sapphira was generous enough, but it wasn't exactly what it appeared to be. It was supposed to represent a total commitment, but it didn't. It may have impressed some of the believers of the early church, but it didn't impress God.

In Jesus we have the perfect example of a proper motive in offerings. His offering to fallen humanity came from the pure motive of inestimable love. His gift wasn't tainted by selfish interests or ulterior motives. But somehow many of the offerings that find their way into the Lord's treasury today fall far short of this standard. Many of them, as a result, are unacceptable.

The Quality of the Tithes and Offerings

In order to better understand the principle of an acceptable offering, one should consider the difference between the tithe and a freewill offering. God entered into a partnership agreement with man. The tithe is His share of the profits made in the management of His goods. In this arrangement, God shares with man both the good and the bad. "And concerning the tithe of the herd, or of the flock, even of whatsoever passeth under the rod, the tenth shall be holy unto the Lord. He shall not search whether it be good or bad, neither shall he change it" (Lev. 27:32, 33). This shows God's fairness in His ordinances.

But the freewill offerings were to be perfect: "And

whosoever offereth a sacrifice of peace offerings unto the Lord to accomplish his vow, or a freewill offering in beeves or sheep, it shall be perfect to be accepted. . . . Ye shall not offer unto the Lord that which is bruised, or crushed, or broken, or cut; neither shall ye make any offering thereof in your land" (Lev. 22:21-24). "In the ancient Jewish service it was required that every sacrifice should be without blemish."—*Counsels on Diet and Foods,* p. 20.

The reprimand that God gave His people in the time of Malachi is usually thought of in connection with the withholding of their tithes and offerings. However, one of God's most scathing rebukes concerned the quality of their offerings: "Ye offer polluted bread upon mine altar; and ye say, Wherein have we polluted thee? In that ye say, The table of the Lord is contemptible. And if ye offer the blind for sacrifice, is it not evil? and if ye offer the lame and sick, is it not evil? offer it now unto thy governor; will he be pleased with thee, or accept thy person? saith the Lord of hosts" (Mal. 1:7, 8).

Does this have an application today? Do God's people offer "polluted bread" on His altar? Consider some offerings that may be "sick" and "lame."

Giving to Emotional Appeals

Too often gifts are made under the emotional stress of "stirring" appeals. When the feelings of the donor return to normal, he feels that he gave too much and regrets that he was "carried away," as it were. Surely such offerings are unacceptable.

> To give or labor when our sympathies are moved, and to withhold our gifts or service when the emotions are not stirred, is an unwise and dangerous course.—*Counsels on Stewardship,* p. 25.

A man was telling his minister one day about the method he and his wife followed in their giving to the church: "My wife and I give as we are impressed." The pastor observed later that from the records it appeared these impressions must have been very weak and at infrequent intervals!

Giving under the influence of feeling can also be

dangerous if the objects to which one gives do not always turn out as expected. The same emotions that prompted the gift can also shut off the flow of benevolence. Acceptable gifts are those that are regular and systematic, *"as God hath prospered,"* gifts that are free from selfish interests and not subject to emotional control. This is disinterested benevolence.

Giving Under Pressure

Giving under pressure will be discussed in detail in a later chapter, but, briefly, it refers to gifts of service or money that are the result of the pressures of social acceptance or financial influence. These offerings are not usually regarded by the donor as gifts at all, but rather as assessments or obligations. They take on a very commercial character not unlike the payments of a contract for merchandise purchased on time.

Giving to Needs

In giving to specific needs, the desirability or urgency of the objective is the motivating force, rather than love for God. Often the giver reacts from a personal interest or a sense of obligation. This causes him to lose sight of the fact that these needs or objectives are an important part of God's work, for which he is responsible as a manager.

In reality, the urgency of the need or the merit of the objective should not be the primary influence that motivates giving. Needs should only be presented as opportunities to give of that which has already been set apart for God in freewill offerings. God's work requires funds. God has placed these in the hands of His stewards. Their devotion to Him will be demonstrated by their willingness to use these resources in His service.

Giving to Win

Quite often, in the heady desire to reach some goal, boys are pitted against the girls, Sabbath school classes against one another, or church against church. Many times the object for which the funds are needed is obscured in competitive promotion and rivalry.

I was seated in a church one day when a goal chart with a large thermometer was placed on an easel. A man spent five minutes or more urging the members to bend every effort to make the red mercury line reach the top—"so that we can go over the goal!" (It appeared from his remarks that the senior division was about to suffer defeat at the hands of the youth.)

Although the amount of the goal was printed in large type at the top of the chart, there was no indication as to what the objective might be. I quietly asked the man seated next to me, "Why are you raising this money?" He whispered back, "To reach the goal!" I never did find out how the money was to be used—I forgot to ask someone else at the close of the service.

Giving to Be Seen

There are those whose giving appears to depend not on the prospering hand of God but upon the accolades of their fellow men. Praise is the magic formula for tapping their wellsprings of benevolence. Jesus spoke of this class when He said, "Take heed that ye do not your alms before men, to be seen of them: otherwise ye have no reward of your Father which is in heaven" (Matt. 6:1). He said that we were to let our light shine—He didn't say we were to shine it into other people's eyes!

Giving to Be Remembered

One of the most successful appeals that can be made, especially for large gifts, is the memorial. Its popularity comes from the desire of the selfish heart to seek recognition for its generosity. Such gifts are not totally given to God, because in the memory of the giver there still remains a part.

In one lovely church, which I shall call the plaque church because there were so many of them, a certain member was rarely mentioned without the supporting reminder, "She's the one who gave the stained-glass window in the front of the church."

When visiting this church one can't help noticing that each window and pew bears the name of the respective giver. It leads one to wonder who gave the bricks under the window sill. How about the floor on which the pews rest? Without these, the windows would have to hang in space and the pews rest upon the ground.

There is an amusing story concerning this desire to give toward specific things. One member was visiting another member in a solicitation program for a new church. The prospective donor said he wouldn't be able to assist with the actual building program because he was going to buy the new organ!

"But we don't need an organ," replied the visitor.

"Why?"

"Because we don't have a church."

"But—you're going to build one, aren't you?"

"I don't think so," was the answer. "Everyone is going to buy organs! So I guess we are just going to have a big pile of organs on our lot."

The man laughed at this absurd picture. Then the visitor kindly suggested, "Look, why don't you help us build the church and we'll help you buy the organ. Then it will be *our* church and *our* organ." The man agreed to this common-sense suggestion.

This principle of everyone working in harmony for a common objective will prevent what happened in another church where the organ was locked up for eighteen months because the man who bought it didn't like the way it was being played!

Giving to Be a Heart Experience

Acceptable offerings are gifts made to God in love and gratitude for His blessings. They are not subject to the personal feelings of the donor regarding the specific objective for which they are used. The accomplishments of human beings are always subject to human error.

Even though the means thus consecrated be misapplied, so that it does not accomplish the object which the donor had in view . . . those who made the sacrifice in sincerity of soul, with an eye single to the glory of God, will not lose their reward.—*Testimonies,* vol. 2, p. 519.

Paul gave the perfect formula for acceptable offerings: "If there *first be a willing mind*" (2 Cor. 8:12), "every man according *as he purposeth in his heart,* so let him give" (2 Cor. 9:7).

These are the only offerings that God will accept—willing gifts from loving hearts, with no strings attached.

The offering from the heart that loves, God delights to honor, giving it highest efficiency.—*The Desire of Ages,* p. 65.

8

SUBSTITUTES FOR PERSONAL SACRIFICE

Any method used to secure funds that is a substitute for personal sacrifice is unacceptable to God.

A selfish heart will go to any length or employ any means for self-protection. The constant search for substitutes for personal sacrifice is not an abnormality of the jet age—it was also common in the age of chariots. Saul, the first king of Israel, gave a classic example.

He was instructed to *utterly* destroy not only the people of Amalek but everything they possessed—"ox and sheep, camel and ass" (1 Sam. 15:3). He almost obeyed the divine command; he saved the king and the "best of the sheep and of the oxen, to sacrifice unto the Lord" (verse 15).

It is possible that some modern "Israelites" would justify this slight deviation by saying, "After all, it was for a good cause!" But God didn't look at it this way. He said, "Behold, to obey is better than sacrifice, and to hearken than the fat of rams" (verse 22). Consider the reason that prompted this sanctimonious desire to save these cattle for sacrifice.

The people reserved for themselves the finest of the flocks, herds, and beasts of burden, excusing their sin on the ground that the cattle were reserved to be offered as sacrifices to the Lord. It was their purpose, however, to use these *merely as a substitute,* to save their own cattle.—*Patriarchs and Prophets,* p. 629. (Italics supplied.)

How many times today God is dishonored by the methods used to secure funds for His work, when they are only substitutes for personal sacrifice. These methods are called "unchristian" and "unhallowed" (*ibid.,* p. 529).

Accepted as Part of Church Life

From observation it would appear that the average churchgoer has been so thoroughly conditioned to an almost endless chain of ideas for raising money that he has come to regard these as a part of his religion. The house of God has been desecrated by promotion and merchandising schemes. Over these Satan throws a religious garment. But every such procedure is a contributing factor to the spiritual delinquency of the church.

The problem most church groups have today is in trying to carry on a worldwide work without disturbing their own selfish interests. They smile complacently when someone suggests "giving until it hurts" or "until it stops hurting," but they show no pain at all when buying unnecessary things for themselves or for their loved ones.

Their sense of values is warped, because deep down inside their hearts the seeds of beneficence are finding the soil flinty and hard. Selfishness has turned the fertile soil into stony ground.

A Vulnerable Point

Probably in no other area of church activity are so many abuses seen as in this area of substitution for personal sacrifice. On this point the church has always been vulnerable. History shows that as more and more funds become necessary in order to carry on the activities of an expanding church, its leaders tend to lose sight of its primary objective. Often its divine mission is buried beneath the rubbish of high-pressure promotion and fund-raising gimmicks.

In ancient and modern history, the church has run the gamut of fund raising for its building, expansion, and maintenance requirements. Every conceivable plan that the selfish minds of men could invent has been used.

Some large churches have been constructed almost entirely from the proceeds of lotteries. At least one was built from pledges secured when the donors' heads were befuddled with wine at a wedding reception! What a terrible contrast between these methods and the ones used in the building of God's house in the wilderness when He instructed Moses, "Of every man that giveth it willingly with his heart ye shall take my offering" (Ex. 25:2).

To support the church and the ministry questionable methods have been used. These include talent programs, rummage sales, commission selling, coupon redemption, insurance plans, merchandising schemes, box socials, pledge systems, breakfasts, dinners, and suppers—and bingo! None of these has brought anything but temporary relief because they are not God's plan for either the maintenance of His church or the support of His ministers.

While some of these plans are associated with the churches of the past century, the same motivations and methods are seen in many of the projects in use today. Frequently the total amount of money is reduced when channeled through these questionable sources, for the selfish human heart always wants something in return.

Giving to Get

There are many individuals who will not willingly give to a noble objective the same amount that they will spend for a dinner, motion picture, or some other form of entertainment in which they will get something for their money. This is the give-to-get motive and is the basis for so many fund-raising schemes. It is the strongest appeal that can be made to the selfish heart.

Instead of appealing to man's reason, to his benevolence, his humanity, his nobler faculties, the most successful appeal that can be made is to the appetite. The gratification of the appetite will induce men to give means when otherwise they would do nothing.—*Selected Messages,* book 2, p. 413.

A few years ago I heard a pastor plead at length for his members to come to the church that Saturday night (at midnight!) to participate in a bus tour that would take them through some beautiful hill country during the fall foliage season. The price of the tour was six dollars, of which three dollars was to be returned to their church building fund by the bus company.

It seemed so strange to me how much sleep these people were willing to lose just to get three dollars into their building fund. *Reason* would dictate that the members should remain in their warm beds, and put the six dollars—or even three—into the fund! But no doubt the pastor knew from experience that they wouldn't *give* unless they also *got* something. This give-to-get motive is the basis for all fund-raising suppers, bake sales, rummage sales, and entertainments.

Innocent (?) Methods

Someone may say that there is no use making a big thing out of a little innocent fun. But a frank and open-minded look at these methods will show the inherent dangers and disastrous results of these substitutes for personal sacrifice.

Even in churches where many of the contemporary methods of fund raising are frowned upon, plans are used that are plants from the same roots.

There seems to be an avalanche of sales promotions by both church and school today. People are constantly "held up" by bright-eyed, rosy-cheeked youngsters selling candy, cookies, and stationery—all for "good causes." Once more, *reason* would say that if the cause is a good one, why not support it with the whole dollar (which is the usual price of the item). Usually about forty cents finds its way into the "cause" and sixty cents goes to some firm that promotes these schemes. Frankly, if such "innocent methods" are strongly urged, at least we can direct our children into worthwhile projects such as magazine sales, or something more beneficial than candy or cookies.

What do these contemporary money-raising methods do to the youth? First, it plants in their minds the idea that objectives can be reached by getting someone else to furnish the money. This does not teach personal involvement and responsibility.

Second, the example of the purchaser is bad because it sows the seeds of *giving to get*. One little fellow seemed nonplused when I assured him that I wanted to help provide playground equipment, but I didn't want the box of candy. He just stood there fingering the dollar bill, trying to figure it all out. Think of the impact on the youth if they were taught to give of their earnings and allowances to projects in which they were interested, and experienced a big assist from adults who had these interests at heart—but didn't need to be bribed for support.

Is the Church a Gambling School?

Even more sinister in its far-reaching results are some of the fairs that are enjoying such current popularity. Into these apparently harmless gatherings is creeping the element of gambling as chances are sold on certain items. A school principal reported that one boy spent five dollars on chances trying to win something that was worth less than half that amount. (His parents can't afford to pay his tuition!)

A little boy came home from one fair, his eyes fairly glittering with excitement. "Daddy!" he cried just as soon as he came through the door. "Daddy! I almost won!" His father, in relating the incident, said, "I never saw that look in the eyes of my son before." How subtly the enemy of souls has infiltrated many church-sponsored activities.

Such an example makes an impression upon the minds of youth. They notice that lotteries and fairs and games are sanctioned by the church, and they think there is something fascinating in this way of obtaining means. . . . He sees the money taken by the one who wins. This looks enticing. It seems an easier way of obtaining money than by earnest work, which requires persevering energy and strict economy. He imagines there can be no harm in this; for similar games have been resorted to in order to obtain means for the benefit of the church. . . . Whether he gains or loses, he is in the downward road to ruin. *But it was the example of the church that led him into the false path.—Counsels on Stewardship,* p. 201. (Italics supplied.)

Many parents who weep bitter tears for their children who have left the church fail to realize that perhaps some of these methods that they used in substitution for personal sacrifice could have been the very means that started them down the wrong road.

All "unhallowed" methods of fund raising tend to lessen respect for the house of God. They lower it to the level of a business establishment or place of amusement and pleasure. Many times the evident lack of reverence can be traced to these activities.

Often the place set apart for God's worship is desecrated by feasting and drinking, buying, selling, and merrymaking. Respect for the house of God and reverence for His worship are lessened in the minds of the youth. The barriers of self-restraint are weakened. Selfishness, appetite, and the love of display, are appealed to, and they strengthen as they are indulged.—*Testimonies,* vol. 9, p. 91.

Funds That Have No Efficiency

Money given from any other motive than the motive of love lacks efficiency, and God cannot bless it. "If I gave everything I have to poor people, and if I were burned alive for preaching the Gospel but didn't love others, it would be of no value whatever" (1 Cor. 13:3, T.L.B.).*

There is no record that Jesus had to be bribed or tempted with food and entertainment in order to get Him to sacrifice for man. If His followers really love Him, their generous impulses will not need to be unhealthfully

---

* From *The Living Bible,* copyright 1971 by Tyndale House Publishers, Wheaton, Ill. Used by permission.

stimulated. They will give continuously and generously because of this love. Such gifts will receive the highest efficiency, for God will not only accept them but bless and multiply them.

Systematic Benevolence the Answer

A lack of necessary funds by a church should be a clear indication that a spiritual revival is needed, not some form of fund raising. Every effort should be put forth to lead each member into a reconsecration of his entire life to God. There should be no money problem in God's church, for He has provided ample resources to carry on the work to which men have been assigned. His plan is simply systematic benevolence.

When everyone is faithful in the return of the tithe and in the giving of freewill offerings, the treasury will be full. This is the formula for a financially successful church and school. No other means should be sought.

If the plan of systematic benevolence were adopted by every individual and fully carried out, there would be a constant supply in the treasury. The income would flow in like a steady stream constantly supplied by overflowing springs of benevolence.—*Ibid.*, vol. 3, pp. 389, 390.

9

THE BUSINESS AND THE RELIGIOUS LIFE

The business life is the religious life in practice.

At church, people can hear what Christians profess; during the week they can see it! Too often church members have two suits—the one they wear during the week, and their "Sabbath clothes." They appear to have two sets of values; one religious, the other business, and they change from one to the other as easily as they change their clothes. Possibly this is because they do not understand the intimate relationship between their religion and their secular employment.

God, speaking to His people through the prophet Isaiah, showed His concern over this separation between a formal religion and a practical one. He recognized their zeal in the Temple services but observed that their daily lives were not a demonstration of their profession. "Is not this the fast that I have chosen? to loose the bands of wickedness, to undo the heavy burdens, and to let the oppressed go free, and that ye break every yoke? Is it not to deal thy bread to the hungry, and that thou bring the poor that are cast out to thy house? when thou seest the naked, that thou cover him; and that thou hide not thyself from thine own flesh?" (Isa. 58:6, 7).

Pure Religion Intensely Practical

James called attention to the importance of a practical religion. "Pure religion and undefiled before God and the Father is this, To visit the fatherless and widows in their affliction, and to keep himself unspotted from the world" (James 1:27). Ellen White commented, "Religion, pure, undefiled religion, is intensely practical."—*Testimonies*, vol. 9, p. 150.

A recognition of and a compliance with the Owner-manager relationship to God would prevent this separation between the religious belief and the business pursuits of life. Unselfish love for God and for one's fellow man would guide every decision, control every transaction.

This idea that there is a separation between the spiritual life and the occupation makes many people reluctant to ask God to bless them in their temporal activities.

A man who was having some difficulty in finding steady employment was asked if he had asked God to help him.

"Do you know what I do?" he asked.

"No."

"I repair old houses. You don't ask God to help you with things like that, do you?"

"What do you ask God for—blessings on the Sabbath school? on the children? on the missionaries?"

"I suppose so."

"Of course you ask God to bless your work—whatever it is—just as long as it is honest. He is vitally interested in whatever you do. You are one of His managers. Wouldn't you be interested in someone who was working for you?"

After this man recognized his active partnership with God, he had more work than he could do—simply because he asked God to bless him and He did. Up to this time he was operating a one-man business, not a partnership with God. The problem is that too many people try too hard to take care of themselves, by themselves. They stumble along through life because they do not avail themselves of the unlimited assistance that God has promised. A recognition of not only our responsibility to God but of *His responsibility to us* would solve many of our problems.

I was invited to a man's house to talk to him about a problem. He was out of work. The situation was made more serious because he was 70 years old, and jobs aren't plentiful for those who have reached their full threescore and ten.

The story of his life was unusual. As a youth he had gone to work for a company and had worked for them all his life until about four years prior to my visit. All his life he had spent at this one job—in the same town! His job was his life, and when he lost it he died a little, inside. He had no pension plan, so he and his wife were forced to depend on what odd jobs they could find.

It was during this trying period that someone invited them to a series of Sunday night meetings in the little church nearby. They gave their hearts to God.

When the pastor explained the tithing system one day, they couldn't see how they could deduct 10 percent from their limited income and still have enough left to care for the barest of necessities. The pastor, however, told them to try it, and if they came to want he would quit preaching!

The man said, "I figured if the preacher would stake his job on it, I'd just as well try. Frankly, we have been better off since we returned the tithe than we were before." He went on to explain, "But I still do not have a steady job, and this is a real problem."

I reminded him that he was one of God's managers— actually in God's employ. Then I asked, "If you were working for me, whose job would it be to tell you what to do?"

"Yours," he said.

"Right. I would tell you when, and where, and what to do. I would be responsible for your wages. What would your part be?"

"An honest day's labor," he replied immediately.

"Don't you see," I went on, "that this is exactly the same relationship you have with God? As your Employer, He is responsible for your employment. Your responsibility is an honest day's labor, or the efficient operation of a business or profession. He has promised to provide for your needs.

"But you must remember the real objective of the work that God will give you. First, it is soul winning. In this employment there will be some soul or souls that you are to reach. You may be able to talk to them, give them literature or Bible studies, or possibly just the example of a Christian life. But you must look for these opportunities. Then, there will be sustenance for both you and your wife."

He rocked back and forth in his chair for a few moments; then his face brightened. "You know," he said, "I believe that!" Just then the phone rang in another room. While he was answering the call, his wife filled us in on some of the details of their financial struggle during the time since he had lost his job. He had become so depressed that she feared for a time that he might attempt to take his life. After they joined the church this was no problem, but somehow he hadn't been the same. Then she said, "When he said, 'I believe that!' I saw the light come back into his eyes."

Both the pastor and I looked to see the "light" in his eyes when he returned, but it must have been something that only his wife could see.

She asked, "Who was it, dear?" He gave a man's name, then explained that he was a farmer just outside town.

"What did he want?" she inquired.

He looked first at her, then at us before replying. Then in a quiet voice—one almost filled with awe—he said, "He just offered me a steady job!"

Soul Winning the Primary Objective

One must remember that Jesus placed special emphasis on our making the kingdom of heaven our first consideration. Food, clothing, and shelter, He said, would come as a result or secondary benefit. This means that in every activity the spread of the gospel message must be the first objective. God places His managers in specific jobs or positions in order to reach souls. There are many ways in which this can be accomplished. The fact that the job or profession will also provide means for the support of the family should be regarded as a secondary objective. Paul made tents, but he isn't remembered for his tentmaking.

One who recognizes his responsibility to God will faithfully carry out all the principles of his religion in a practical application in his business or occupation. *His work will be his religion.*

A doctor in Africa, who was semiretired, opened two small offices in communities about forty miles on either side of the city in which he resided. He did this because there was no medical service available in these areas and most of the people, being very poor, found it difficult to get into the city.

Because the offices were open only one day each week, the number who came for help was very small and he was about to close them when he caught this "primary objective" idea—the real aim for his profession.

He started to pray, not for opportunities to render medical assistance, but for opportunities to share the good news of salvation. The results were immediate. Each office was filled from morning to night on the days he visited them. His opportunities to witness were unlimited. It seemed everyone who came not only needed medical attention but was eager to listen to his advice for better living, and to hear the wonderful news of a loving God and the home He was preparing where sickness would be unknown.

His face shone with elation as he told of this experience. He concluded, "When I finally realized *why* I am a doctor, and *what* my profession really is, then God could work a miracle through me. Now I know that my profession is my religion in practice."

"When we devote ourselves to the affairs of the kingdom of God, He will mind our affairs."—*Our High Calling,* p. 196. This is pure religion—a practical partnership with God in every occupation, in every profession.

10

THE DANGER IN PROSPERITY

The danger in prosperity is its inherent tendency to lessen or erase a man's dependence upon God.

"'Oh, if I only had means, I would not squander it! I would set an example to those who are close and penurious. I would show them the great blessing there is to be received in doing good.'"—*Testimonies,* vol. 2, p. 277.

This statement was made by a woman who loved the Lord but because of her poverty was able to give only small offerings. As she saw those around her who were prosperous but who did little for the cause of God, she envied them their wealth.

God said to His angel that ministered to her: "'I have proved her in poverty and affliction, and she has not separated herself from Me, nor rebelled against Me. I will now prove her with prosperity. I will reveal to her a page of the human heart with which she is unacquainted. I will show her that money is the most dangerous foe she has ever met. I will reveal to her the deceitfulness of riches; that they are a snare, even to those who feel that they are secure from selfishness."—*Ibid.,* p. 278.

There was a complete reversal in this woman's fortunes.

Now everything she touched seemed to turn to gold. What did she do? The account goes on to say, "When you had a home you saw so many improvements to make to have everything about you convenient and pleasant that you forgot the Lord and His claims upon you, and were less inclined to help the cause of God than in the days of your poverty and affliction."—*Ibid.*, p. 283.

Of Divine Origin

The desire to be healthy and wealthy is of divine origin. God intended that His people of all ages were to be an object lesson to the entire world because of these characteristics. Everyone with whom they would come in contact would ask the source of their blessings. These could then be directed to God, the Provider of every good and perfect gift.

Think of the strategic position in which God placed the Israelites. In a land "flowing with milk and honey," at the crossroads of the world, they were to be a spectacle to every traveler. Let us imagine the conversation of a traveler from the East as he speaks to his host in one of the local motels:

"There's something that's bothering me," he begins.

"What is it?" inquires his host.

"Well, first, the people. In all my travels I have never seen such happy, healthy people as you. And then the crops. Never have I seen anything like it—not even in the land of Goshen down in Egypt. How do you account for it?"

"Well, you see, sir, it's because of our God."

"Gods!" the man laughs, spreading his hands wide apart. "We have dozens of them, but they don't do anything for us—not like this!"

"But that's just the point," earnestly explains the host. "Our God is the true God, Jehovah. He isn't like your gods. He's a living God. He brought us into this land and promised that if we would obey His instruction, we would always be healthy, our lands would be fertile, and we would never lack for anything. You know, He even gives us the right amount of rain at the right time—just when we need it!"

"Please tell me more about your God. I think we need Him back home."

And so the Israelites were given the opportunity of spreading the story of God and His love all around the world—without ever leaving home. This was God's plan for them, and it included health and prosperity in order to attract people.

Heaven's Salesmen

God has planned an unlimited number of thousand-year vacations to be available in heaven—and a great deal of real estate on the new earth. The only agents He has are His followers; the only advertising, their lives. They are His "salesmen." If these salesmen are to be successful in convincing others of the desirability of heaven and the new earth, they must look, talk, act, and be successful. This is one reason why God planned for all His people to be prosperous.

In addition, we are His children—the sons and daughters of a King. He wants us to have the best of everything. Peter understood the lofty plans God has for His people: "But ye are a chosen generation, a royal priesthood, an holy nation, a peculiar people; *that ye should shew forth* the praises of him who hath called you out of darkness into his marvellous light" (1 Peter 2:9).

Self-sufficiency

However, there are potential dangers in prosperity. Chief among these is the feeling of self-sufficiency that the possession of wealth brings. As wealth increases, the feeling of dependence on God tends to decrease. The mind seems to accept the idea that every need, every desire, can be acquired or satisfied with money. This is pure folly.

There is nothing in this world that is not subject to loss. Fire, flood, and wars have wiped out fortunes that took lifetimes to accumulate. Obsolescence has destroyed the dreams and labors of years, overnight. It is sheer insanity to place one's confidence and dependence upon man or anything man-made. Only a creative God can control the forces of nature or overrule the machinations of men. Only God can guarantee security.

God implanted the desire for prosperity for noble ends. John Wesley taught that a man should *earn* all he could and *save* all he could, so that he could *give* all he could. Prosperity among God's people was designed to furnish them with abundant means to effectually carry out the great work to which they were assigned.

The Desire to Hoard

There is another danger in prosperity, the almost overwhelming urge to hoard riches against some possible future need. While the Christian is well-advised to lay aside an emergency fund for a "rainy day," he is never to hoard. It should be for a "rainy day," not for a hurricane!

The principles of heaven are based on continual exchange—receiving and imparting. Hoarding stops the flow of exchange.

When Christians are controlled by the principles of heaven, they will dispense with one hand, while the other gains. This is the only rational and healthy position a Christian can occupy while having and still making money.—*Ibid.*, p. 240.

Gratification of Self

Then there is the danger of self-gratification. A prosperous businessman, who in his youth was a member of the church, was having lunch with a friend in one of the fashionable hotels of a large city. The friend tried to question him discretely about his religious life now that he had reached the pinnacle of success as measured by worldly standards.

"I have a Cadillac in the parking lot, a Mercedes and a Jaguar in the garage at home. I live in a five-hundred-thousand-dollar house. I have stocks, bonds, and a guaranteed income. Why do I need God?"

The wisest man who ever lived, and surely one of the most wealthy, wrote, "Give me neither poverty nor riches; feed me with food convenient for me: lest I be full, and deny thee, and say, Who is the Lord? or lest I be poor, and steal, and take the name of my God in vain" (Prov. 30:8, 9).

It is not the empty cup that we have trouble in carrying; it is the cup full to the brim that must be carefully balanced. . . . It is prosperity that is dangerous to spiritual life.—*Counsels on Stewardship,* p. 148.

Prosperity Can Be a Blessing

Though there is great danger in prosperity, there are safeguards that can make it a great blessing.

First, if one recognizes the fact that he is actually a manager of God's goods, he will handle these possessions as God would handle them if He were managing His own. The gratification of self will not prove to be an overpowering temptation when one recognizes this relationship.

You are bidden to enjoy the good gifts of the Lord, and should use them for your own comfort, for charitable purposes, and in good works to advance His cause, thereby laying up for yourself treasures in heaven.—*Testimonies,* vol. 4, p. 143.

Second, one must guard his desires. Joshua called for the Israelites to make a choice one day. "Choose you this day whom ye will serve," he challenged, "whether the gods which your fathers served that were on the other side of the flood, or the gods of the Amorites, in whose land ye dwell" (Joshua 24:15).

We dwell in a land where the "gods of the Amorites" glitter from every sales lot and every store window. We are continually bombarded with appeals to gratify self. We live in a gimmick world. But every person has the power to choose. And he *must* choose. There can be no compromise. "If any man love the world, the love of the Father is not in him. For all that is in the world, the lust of the flesh, and the lust of the eyes, and the pride of life, is not of the Father, but is of the world" (1 John 2:15, 16).

Third, benevolence must keep pace with the prosperity. By dispensing as one receives, a person can become an open channel for God. The more one has, the bigger the channel he can become. Thus the unlimited resources of heaven can flood the earth.

By exercise, benevolence constantly enlarges and strengthens, until it becomes a principle and reigns in the soul. It is highly dangerous to spirituality to allow selfishness and covetousness the least room in the heart.—*Ibid.,* vol. 3, pp. 548, 549. (Italics supplied.)

The Bible leaves us the record of a man who it says was "the greatest of all the men of the east." It records the enormous wealth of the man, Job. He understood his responsibility to God. "I was eyes to the blind," he testified, "and feet was I to the lame. I was a father to the poor: and the cause which I knew not I searched out" (Job 29:15, 16).

Finally, before a person expresses his desire to be rich, he should carefully consider the dangers in prosperity. It is no sin to be rich, but, oh, so dangerous!

11

THE DANGER IN SPECULATION

The danger in speculation is the feverish desire that it creates to make profits faster than normal conditions will permit—or to get something for nothing.

The world has always had its get-rich-quick schemes. Even the prophet Balaam fell victim to one of these. The life savings of elderly people have figuratively developed wings and flown away in their desire to double, triple, or quadruple their money. Whole fortunes have been won and lost because of the intoxicating thrill of *speculation*. However, almost the same statements can be made regarding *investment*. What, then, is the difference?

Investment Praised

In some cases there appears to be a very fine distinction between speculation and investment. But there is a difference. The Bible certainly does not condemn investment. On the contrary, it is encouraged as a means of increasing the size of one's management. In the parable of the talents the men who doubled their investments were praised and their responsibilities increased. Only the man who did nothing was condemned.

Solomon, observing that a virtuous woman is above the

price of rubies, said that among her other qualities would be that of a wise investor—in this instance buying a field and planting a vineyard. And so, from the many references to it, it would seem that investment is one of the definite responsibilities of a Christian manager—another phase in the management of life.

Investment appears to be a business enterprise that is based on sound economic principles of normal supply and demand. The woman who planted the vineyard had every right to expect that there would be a market for her grapes. She had every reason to anticipate a normal rate of growth from her vineyard and a corresponding margin of profit. This was true investment.

Speculation Condemned

In speculation, the growth sought and profits anticipated is abnormal—or greater than existing conditions usually permit. Solomon observed, "A faithful man shall abound with blessings: but he that *maketh haste* to be rich shall not be innocent" (Prov. 28:20). Ellen White comments, "I was shown that it is a dangerous experiment for our people to engage in speculation. They thereby place themselves on the enemy's ground, subject to great temptations, disappointments, trials, and losses. Then comes a *feverish unrest,* a longing desire *to obtain means more rapidly* than present circumstances will admit."—*Testimonies,* vol. 4, p. 617. (Italics supplied.)

The abnormal growths usually associated with speculation are often the results of chance, calculated manipulation, or the adversity or misfortune of other people. Many times the excessive profits are made possible by a critical lack of supply coupled with an unusual demand.

The story is told of a man who saw an unusual opportunity for speculation just following the great San Francisco earthquake. Before the fires had been quenched and while the populace was still in a state of shock, he leased a large vacant space, then rushed out of town and took options on large supplies of lumber and building materials. He now had a substantial corner on the available market.

The demand for building supplies was immediate and desperate. By charging exorbitant prices, he became so wealthy that after this one venture he was able to retire. For the rest of his life he lived off the interest on the money he made in this one speculation. For his own selfish interests he took advantage of the misfortunes of his fellow men by adding to their already inescapable burdens.

Something for Nothing

The profits received from a successful speculation are also detrimental because they are not the result of a normal expenditure of energy and honest labor.

A man who had been very successful in "playing" the stock market helped his 19-year-old son to become involved by "showing him the ropes." The first year this boy, who was still in school, is reported to have made nearly sixty thousand dollars! Will this boy ever be satisfied with normal, honest labor? This is at least open to question. Parents have been advised, "The very best legacy which parents can leave their children is a knowledge of useful labor and the example of a life characterized by disinterested benevolence."—*Ibid.*, vol. 3, p. 399.

Instead of a "knowledge of useful labor," his father has sown the seeds of easy profit without labor in the mind of his son, and he may live to regret this action.

In reality, there is no difference between the fortunes won at the card table, at the horse race, or in the fluctuation of a speculative stock (the price of which has little or no direct relationship to the sale of the products it represents, but rather to its own popularity and demand). In each case no tangible asset is involved except the money used to buy some chips; a win, place, or show ticket; or a gilt-edged certificate.

God said, "Six days shalt thou labour." This refers to the healthy expenditure of energy in the production of something that will be beneficial to mankind. But speculation is usually associated with idleness and leisure because one reason for speculation is to free the individual from labor. Idleness and luxury have always been associated with indulgence, dissipation, and vice.

The Possibility of Loss

Then there is the probability of loss in speculation. Thousands have been duped out of their money by fast-talking promoters who can rival the great Houdini in disappearing after their prospect has been "fleeced."

Money received for honest labor represents a portion of a man's very life—the portion he expended in making it. Certainly God would not want this monetary representation of a person's life hazarded on the turn of a card, the speed of a horse, the caprice of some glamour stock, or a piece of speculative real estate.

Often one reads in the investor's section of the newspaper of someone who has been left a sum of money, inquiring whether it is safe to invest it in some speculative, fast-growth stock. The answer is always the same, "If you can't afford to lose it, you can't afford to *gamble!*"

Gamble? This facet of speculation makes it doubly dangerous for the Christian manager. While he might never be found entering a gaming room or attending a horse race, the same spirit of gambling is the basis of speculation. The spirit of chance is not the spirit of heaven. The Christian is warned against it in every form.

One man had saved a few thousand dollars that he intended to use as a down payment on a home for his family. He was advised by an acquaintance to put this money in a "sure-fire" speculation. "Why fool around with a down payment," he was asked, "when you can get the whole house for nothing?" In a very short time he lost every cent of the money that had been accumulated at such sacrifice and frugality. "How I wish," he told a friend, "that I had put the whole amount into God's work. Now I have lost it. How can I account for it?"

It is true that one might lose in some legitimate enterprise because of conditions over which he has no control. The hazards are many in this world for even the most careful of investors; but to take a chance in speculation is to invite loss.

The real threat in speculation, then, is the motive that prompts it—the desire to get something for nothing, or the desire to make money faster than normal conditions will admit. In either winning or losing, the spirit that it generates has a blasting effect on mind, body, and soul.

12

A MANAGER'S RESPONSIBILITY AFTER DEATH

A person is still accountable for his trust, even after death—unless he has made proper arrangements for its transfer.

A Christian mother, disregarding the instruction given in regard to leaving money to non-Christian children, left fifty thousand dollars to her son at her death. She reasoned that when he saw how much she loved him he would return to the church of his childhood. He used the money to buy a beer parlor!

Is she accountable for the wrong use of this money? Only a just God, who understands the motives, knows the answer. However, this incident presents a field for thought. This woman, who had an intense hatred for liquor (her husband died an alcoholic) could have prevented the misuse of the funds entrusted to her by God if she had followed His instructions. This is another example of the unfortunate results of following one's own wisdom.

Two Standards

It appears strange that people seem to use a different set of standards when dealing with one another than when dealing with God. It must be because they do not recognize

God's ownership. When a person recognizes this fact he seems to have no difficulty in determining the right course of action.

A wheat farmer in Montana found the principles of life management rather perplexing until they were put in a local setting with which he was familiar.

"Let's suppose," he was told, "that someone purchased a large ranch in this area and hired you as the foreman. How would you run the ranch?"

"Why," he replied without hesitation, "just as near to the owner's wishes as I possibly could. All the minor decisions I would take care of, but just as close as I could to what I thought he would want. If there were any major decisions to be made, I'd contact him for instructions."

"Now, what would you do," he was asked, "if you suddenly found you were going to die and you couldn't contact the owner because he was off in some corner of the world on a trip?"

He thought for a moment, then said, "I'd make the best arrangements I could to see that the ranch was cared for until he returned and could make other arrangements."

This man had a perfect understanding of the principles involved in a situation between people. Now he could see the parallel between this and a God-and-man relationship. The problem once more is a question of ownership.

There are those who appear to recognize this relationship when living, but fail to apply the same principles when making provision for their entrusted goods after death. Possibly this attitude is a result of the practice of referring to a person's trust as "your estate," or to the disposition of "your property."

There are some definite guidelines for the disposition of one's trust after death. The first of these has to do with the distribution of property while living.

Dying Charity

Jesus said to lay up treasure in heaven where it would be safe from moths, rust, and thieves. It is utter folly to defer this investment until nearly the last moment of life. It isn't the "big deposit" that wins heaven's approval, but the daily acts of benevolence throughout the lifetime. "Dying charity is a poor substitute for living benevolence."—*Testimonies, vol. 5, p. 155.*

The faithful manager will continually distribute the blessings that are channeled through him. Such a course will greatly lessen the danger in the final disposition of his trust, because he won't have so much left to distribute.

A Proper Disposition

A person should always have his business in such a shape that he can leave it at any time, knowing that it will be settled as he would wish were he handling the matter himself. To do this, a will or trust agreement should be carefully drawn that will stand the test of law.

Those who make their wills should not spare pains or expense to obtain legal advice and to have them drawn up in a manner to stand the test.—*Ibid.,* vol. 3, p. 117.

Be Careful in Leaving Large Sums to Children

God knows exactly how much each individual can manage wisely. If an indulgent parent leaves his children a large sum of money, he actually assumes a role that belongs to God alone. He, instead of God, is determining the ability. Many times the leaving of large sums to children has proved to be a curse rather than a blessing.

One man related that when he was 21 years old, his father gave him $100,000! He spent it all before he was 25. Each of his brothers and a sister received a like amount. Not one of them had any of this money by the age of 30. God has said, "The very best legacy which parents can leave their children is a knowledge of useful labor and the example of a life characterized by disinterested benevolence."—*Ibid.,* p. 399.

Parents should seek earnestly for divine wisdom in this matter. They should exercise godly caution in leaving their children more than is necessary for their Christian education, and for their care to the age of maturity. They must never hoard means in order to leave a large legacy to the children.

"Parents should have great fear in entrusting children with the talents of means that God has placed in their hands, unless they have the surest evidence that their children have greater interest in, love for, and devotion to, the cause of God than they themselves possess."—*Ibid.*, p. 118.

Do Not Follow Custom

There are those who dispose of their final trusts as if these were their own, following the custom of leaving it to children and a long list of relatives and friends who do not need it. The principle that should guide their decision is that it all belongs to God. How would He want it distributed? If all property is on the altar of sacrifice, and one earnestly seeks for wisdom, the Lord has promised to reveal His will in this matter.

Ways to Transfer Management

Sometimes there are aged or infirm relatives or friends who should be remembered. To transfer a portion of one's management to these worthy ones would certainly be according to God's instruction.

Then, in planning for the disposition of one's trust, God's cause should always be considered. He has entrusted men with means to enable them to carry the good news of salvation to the world. In no better way could a person transfer his responsibility than to return his stewardship through the agencies of the church. This would put it directly back into God's hands, totally under His direction.

Do Not Bury It in the "Cause"

There is a tendency on the part of some to "bury" their money in the "cause." They enter into revocable trusts with the conference organization, involving large sums of money. They expect the going rate of interest, and although they still retain full control of these funds, they feel that the money is being used in the Lord's work. Many use this excuse when approached for assistance for church and school buildings.

The conferences cannot use these funds to carry on the Lord's work, for they must be instantly available should the trustor so require.

At one time the conferences could invest these funds at a higher rate of interest than was paid the trustor and the difference could be used in the Lord's work. In many areas today this is forbidden by law—thus the conference becomes an investment broker for the trustor without being able to charge for its services.

No reference is being made here to those small estates that are held in trust against the future support and possible illness of elderly people. These are "rainy day" trusts—not surplus funds being hidden in the church.

The great principle to consider in the making of wills and trust agreements is that all property belongs to God and is therefore to be handled in accordance with His wishes. Under these provisions, a faithful manager may relinquish his responsibility at death. Death, in this case, will only be a rest period before he is given the management of eternal, imperishable wealth—because he will have proved to be a faithful manager in this world.

"And I heard a voice from heaven saying unto me, Write, Blessed are the dead which die in the Lord from henceforth: Yea, saith the Spirit, that they may rest from their labours; and their works do follow them" (Rev. 14:13).

13

PLANNED GIVING

Giving to God should be as carefully planned and as systematic as His gifts to us.

The springs of benevolence are like springs of water—the more they are used, the more continuous they will flow. But if they are never used, or become clogged with debris, they tend to dry up. This principle is as true in the spiritual life as it is in the natural. Sometimes the wellsprings of benevolence do not flow freely because of emotional or impulse giving.

God supplies the mountain springs with rain and snow that they may water the fields below. Just so, He fills the hands of His people with whatever is required for their sustenance and for their work in the saving of souls. This continual receiving and imparting is shown in this statement:

Give what you can now, and as you cooperate with Christ, your hand will open to impart still more. And *God will refill your hand,* that the treasure of truth may be taken to many souls. He will give to you that you may give to others.—*Counsels on Stewardship,* p. 50. (Italics supplied.)

God's Voice in the Income

In nature there is a continual receiving and imparting. Christian benevolence must follow this same pattern. The key to acceptable, systematic giving is found in this quotation:

> If spiritually awake, they would hear in the income of every week, whether much or little, *the voice of God.*"—*Testimonies*, vol. 4, p. 474. (Italics supplied.)

It is doubtful that many Christians have ever really listened to God's voice speaking in their incomes. No doubt they hear His voice at other times and in other places, but rarely does one expect to hear God speaking in such an unlikely place as in the income.

The voices usually heard in the income are those associated with trying to keep up with the expenses of daily living. Then there are other voices—constant, nagging voices—the incessant appeal of the advertiser, the urging of the selfish heart. But God's voice in the income? This is rarely heard, and still it is the answer to all the perplexities and unrest that so often plague the soul. A little time spent listening to Him speak would save hours and hours of worry and concern.

Wrong Giving Patterns

Observation of family giving patterns reveals some interesting behavior. Many do it this way:

    1. NEEDS

    2. WANTS   > Me

    3. TITHE

    4. OFFERING   > God

It is assumed that in this instance the needs are real, the wants within reason, the tithe honest, and the offerings generous. But still there is something basically wrong with this order of distribution of the income—the problem is that God has been placed last on the list.

In Isaiah, chapter forty-four, there is an interesting

story of a heathen man who planted an ash tree. God watered it and it grew. One day the man cut it down, built himself a fire, cooked his meal, and warmed himself. "Aha," he said, "I am warm, I have seen the fire" (Isa. 44:16).

But somehow he wasn't quite satisfied, so out of the residue he made a god. Then he bowed down to this little image made from a scrap and said, "Deliver me; for thou art my god" (verse 17). The immediate reaction of any enlightened person is amazement at this utter stupidity.

And still, how much difference is there between a professing Christian and this heathen if the Christian's God also comes last, if God gets only what is left over? God must be first—in every thought, in every action. This is the first commandment, the law of the universe.

Then there are those who manage (?) their incomes this way:

1. WANTS
2. NEEDS
3.   ?
4.   ?

One of the devil's most successful snares is in the area of wants. The world is filled with things that are desirable. Each person is subject to a continual bombardment of advertising—all designed to get him to buy things. John warned of this danger when he wrote, "Love not the world, neither the things that are in the world. If any man love the world, the love of the Father is not in him. For all that is in the world, the lust of the flesh, and the lust of the eyes, and the pride of life, is not of the Father, but is of the world" (1 John 2:15, 16). But the love of things, even those beyond their reach, is overpowering to many people. These become a trap from which there is little chance of escape.

God's Method

Then there is a clearly defined plan for the use of the income:

1. TITHE
2. OFFERING ——> God
3. NEEDS
4. WANTS ——> Me

First— "They would hear in the income . . . the voice of God."—*Testimonies*, vol. 4, p. 474.

Second—"Before any portion is consumed, we should set apart that which God has specified as His."—*Counsels on Stewardship*, p. 81.

Third— "After the tithe is set apart, let gifts and offerings be apportioned, 'as God hath prospered' you."—*Counsels on Sabbath School Work*, p. 130.

Some Christian families have started listening to God's voice in their incomes through a program they call Family Time. Here is how it works:

Family Time

When the family income is received, whether it be weekly, bimonthly, or monthly, a time is set aside when just the family gathers around the table for Family Time. The income is placed in the center of the table. (Note: This could be a token amount representing the income, but with enough to give each child his allowance. The balance of the income—if banked when received—could be represented by an amount on a slip of paper. The tithe and offerings could be set apart by writing a check.)

Listen as the father speaks:

"Children, this money came from God. He gave me the skill and talent to earn it and provided me with a job. My, how thankful we should be! There are families in the world—many of them—who do not have houses like ours, nor clothes like ours, and many of them are cold and hungry. Let us hold hands around the table and thank God for all the things He has given to us."

The family listens as he thanks God for the income. After prayer, he says, "We are told that we should hear

God's voice speaking in this income. If we listen very quietly, what do you suppose we will hear?"

Everyone listens for a moment, then he continues:

"I know the first thing I can hear. God says that He is in partnership with us. His share of this partnership is 10 percent of our increase or profits. So the first thing we must do is put God's share over here by itself. This is the tithe."

He sets the tithe to one side (or figures it and places the amount on a slip of paper if a check is to be written covering both the tithe and offerings).

"And you know, children, we are never to use this money—not even in an emergency. If we did, then that would show that we didn't trust God, for He has said that He will make this amount that is left worth more than the entire amount if we faithfully return His portion to Him. So you see, God has already performed a miracle. This amount that is left is now worth more than it was before I took out God's portion.

"God tells us that we won't have to worry about food, or clothes, or a shelter. Jesus promised that all these things would be provided for us if we are faithful. Isn't that wonderful?

"What else do you suppose God will tell us in our income? Probably He will remind us of all the people in the world who are without food, and clothes, and houses. There are millions who have never heard the good news that Jesus is coming—in fact, they don't know Jesus at all. So God says, 'I wish you would help these poor folks because they are My children, too, just like you are. You can give an offering to Me and I will use it to provide them with food, clothing, and shelter, and to send missionaries to tell them about Me.' Isn't it wonderful that God lets us work for Him?"

This should be an interesting and vivid recital of the needs of the world, using both local and mission stories as illustrations. At this time the family accounts are figured and subtracted from the income. Now a freewill offering is laid aside for God. This will be distributed by the family to local and world needs when the family attends church.

Opportunity for Child Education

This study of family finance provides a wonderful opportunity to teach the children (possibly the adult members, as well) economy. For instance, if the light bill seems unusually high, attention can be called to the fact that if the family were more careful in turning off the lights in rooms not being used, there would be more to give to Jesus. Other habits of economy can also be emphasized. As God's voice speaks in the income, the entire family becomes more aware of its responsibility—its wants will be kept under control.

Each child is now given his allowance and taught how to figure the tithe. After the tithe is set apart, he can set apart his offerings. This is in harmony with inspired instruction:

> They [the children] should not be satisfied to take money from their father or mother and put it into the treasury as an offering, when it is not theirs. They should say to themselves, "Shall I give of that which costs me nothing?"—*The Adventist Home*, p. 387.

Too often children do not form habits of tithing and the giving of freewill offerings. The parent gives them the money for their offerings. They do not tithe either their allowances or small earnings. They need the experience of managing that which has been entrusted to them. This training in Family Time will provide opportunity for them to develop right habits early in life. These will persist with them throughout the years.

Not only will a program such as Family Time be following God's instruction, but it will prove to be valuable in teaching children other principles in the handling of money. They should be taught economy (*Child Guidance*, p. 134), how to save (*Testimonies*, vol. 9, p. 55), how to keep their accounts (*Child Guidance*, p. 136), and how to purchase their clothing (*ibid.*).

Frequent reports from families that are following this program show that it is an enjoyable and memorable occasion—one to which the children look forward. One mother said, "We have never had such an experience before in our family. When I listened to my husband explaining to the children how God was speaking to us in our incomes, I was thrilled beyond comparison. God seemed to be right there at the table with us."

After one Family Time session, the 12-year-old son came to his father privately and said, "Dad, I didn't know it cost so much to take care of the family. I want to give part of my allowance back to you." When the father explained that he should keep his allowance because it was all planned this way, the boy insisted, "But, Dad, you have to work hard. Won't you please let me help you care for the family?"

If every Christian listened to God speaking in his income, he would be led to say something similar to what this boy said: "Father, I didn't realize how much it cost You to care for the family. I know You sent Your only Son to die for us, but I didn't really realize how much it cost. Won't You please let me help You care for the family?" With such an attitude, giving would never seem to be a duty at all, but willing assistance. This was God's plan for financing His work—divine beneficence continually flowing through the human agent to a needy world.

Distributing God's Part

Now that the tithes and offerings have been set apart for God at home, they must be distributed, and this can be done at church. The tithe is placed in the offering envelope and recorded in the space provided. The offerings must be divided between local offerings and world offerings.

Local offerings: If the church is operating on a church budget plan, this offering can be placed in the envelope under this designation. This means that these funds will be distributed by the church treasurer to cover all the needs of the church. If the church is not operating under such a plan, then this fund must be distributed to the specific needs such as church expense, Sabbath school expense, Dorcas, church school budget, et cetera.

World offerings: This portion should be distributed to specific world offerings such as Sabbath school offerings, mission offerings, evangelizing periodical campaigns, and special appeals.

Advantages of Plan

What are the advantages of a planned-giving program?

First, it forms habits of systematic and continuous giving.

Second, it provides a constant reminder of God's ownership. God is the philanthropist, man but the agent.

Third, it provides an available source of funds from which to draw whenever opportunities are presented for helping those in need, or aiding in the spread of the cause of truth.

Fourth, by giving to God instead of to things, it frees one from the danger of allowing the feelings to stop the flow of benevolence should circumstances occur that are not exactly to the individual liking. This is referred to as "disinterested benevolence," which is never influenced or controlled by impulse or feeling.

Fifth, continual giving starves covetousness to death. Selfishness is said to be the greatest sin in the church today. Systematic giving, from a recognition of the Owner-manager principle, will provide a safeguard to the entire family against this dread malady.

Sixth, there is the feeling of satisfaction that comes from an active recognition of a partnership with God. A professional man who practices planned giving recently said, "You know, God has more in His account than I have in mine—and that's the way I want it."

I saw that in the arrangement of systematic benevolence, hearts will be tested and proved. It is a constant, living test. It brings one to understand his own heart, to see whether the truth or the love of the world predominates. Here is a test for the naturally selfish and covetous.—*Testimonies*, vol. 1, p. 221.

14

A MAN'S POTENTIAL

A man's potential cannot be measured by the size of his trust, but by his willingness to use it as God directs.

"We've scraped the bottom of the barrel!" was the remark of the man over the telephone as he tried to explain the financial dilemma of his church. "Whose barrel?" he was asked. "Surely not God's, for there isn't any bottom in His barrel!"

Man has always had a tendency to measure his potential by his own balance sheet. He adds up how much the task requires, then adds up his resources, and often comes up short—especially in God's work. This is because God never gave a plan to mankind that looked reasonable from the human viewpoint—and He did it on purpose. The human heart seems to thrive on honor or praise. If God furnished people with everything in advance to accomplish His work, they would take the credit for its accomplishment.

Dependence on God Essential

So God arranged His work so that people have to depend on Him for its success. This is the only way He can direct a person's attention away from this world and himself. We cannot lift ourselves by our bootstraps, although at times we try. Our aspirations will never be any higher than our narrow, limited concept, unless we direct our thoughts upward to God and learn to think in the context of heaven. Therefore, God's plans for us have always been those of a partnership—a partnership in which there are no limits. Traveling through Canada, one sees many business signs with the abbreviation "Ltd." following the firm name, which means that it is a company in which the liabilities of the shareholders are limited. In God's firm it is "God and Man—Unlimited."

One time there was a poor widow who found herself in a desperate financial situation. Her husband, a preacher, had died, leaving some debts that she was unable to pay. One day the men holding the notes came to see her and, on learning that she had no money, were about to take her two sons as payment. All she could do was beg for a little time, which they reluctantly granted.

She went to a prophet of God and he asked her what assets she had. She replied, "Thine handmaid hath not any thing in the house, save a pot of oil" (2 Kings 4:2). Most people would have thrown up their hands at this and advised her to declare bankruptcy. But the prophet was not dismayed. He told her to borrow all the empty vessels she could from her neighbors, and cautioned her not to "borrow a few." Then he said she was to close the door and start pouring!

One can imagine her amazement as gallon after gallon of oil came from that little pot. Finally all the vessels in the room were full. There she stood with the little pot in her hand and told her son to bring another one. "There aren't any more, Mother," he replied. The record says, "And the oil stayed."

Another time a man brought some loaves of barley and roasting ears as a present for the prophet. When the prophet told his servitor to set the table and serve the food he said, "What, should I set this before an hundred men?" The prophet said, "They shall eat, and shall leave thereof" (2 Kings 4:43).

In the Hands of God

Note carefully a phrase in this question: "The supply in their hands may seem to fall short of the need to be filled; but *in the hands of the Lord* it will prove more than sufficient."—*Prophets and Kings*, p. 243. (Italics supplied.)

It was only a small vessel of oil in the hands of the poor widow, but in the hands of the Lord . . . ! A few small loaves of bread and some roasting ears didn't look like much to set before a hundred men, but . . . ! The little boy's lunch was only some biscuits and a few small fish until Jesus took them in His hands, but what a potluck dinner that turned out to be!

This principle can be illustrated in this way:

Total Objective According to God's Plan

Man's Part   God's Part

"In the hands of the Lord it will prove *more* than sufficient."

The company of believers wasn't very large, but they had outgrown the little church in which they worshiped. They had plans for the building of a new sanctuary. I was invited to come and explain the great principles of life management, and how these applied to the building of a house for God.

Shortly after arriving in the little town, I heard the disturbing news that one of the members, a physician, was planning to leave. He had been a real mainstay in this church with his dedicated service and his financial support. For just a moment I was stunned by the news—then I recovered, remembering that "in the hands of the Lord . . ." I asked my informant if the church folk had heard the news yet. He said he didn't think so—but it was easy to see they had by the time of the evening meeting!

The looks on their faces would have been appropriate for a funeral, but certainly not for entering into the glorious experience of planning a house for God.

By the way of introduction to the subject, I said, "So, you're going to build a church!"

"How can we?" glumly remarked one of the members. "Haven't you heard the news?"

"What news?" I pretended not to know.

"Why, the news that Dr. ——— is leaving!"

"What does that have to do with building a church?" I inquired.

"Why—everything!" The reply was a chorus.

"Oh?" I asked. "Do you mean to say that God can't build a church here without the good doctor? My! My! You don't understand God. Why, He could build a church if there were just one poor widow, or for that matter without even a poor widow. God doesn't have to depend on anyone for His work. He just allows us to help Him, that's all."

Their faces brightened as the gloom of discouragement, which Satan always tries to throw over those with a small potential, was dispelled.

"What should we do?" they asked.

I drew a simple diagram (see page 96) on the blackboard and explained that God expects us to go only as far as we can—the amount makes no difference just as long as we move out to the limit of our capacity. When we reach this limit then He takes over and makes up for any lack that we may have.

Then I asked if they were willing to follow this formula, and they said they were. Someone wanted to know how long it would take to build a church. Estimating their potential based on their annual tithe, I told them nine years. They said they didn't want to wait that long. I told them that they probably wouldn't have to, but I couldn't say for sure because I didn't know what God had in mind for them.

The pastor told me from time to time of their progress. They were all working in unity as hard as they could. God really blessed these people, and in three years they had given twice as much as the human estimate indicated they could. This still was only half of what they needed for a new church. Then God made His move.

In town lived a certain elderly widow. One day she became ill and was taken to the community hospital. As the nurse took her record she asked, "To what church do you belong?" The widow replied, "I'm a Seventh-day Adventist." (No one in the church had any knowledge of her interest at all.)

After a short illness, she passed away. The pastor was called to the office of a lawyer, where her will was read. Having no living kin, she had left a large sum of money and her house and lot to the church! After the house was sold and this amount added to the cash bequest, the amount exactly equaled the three-year giving of the membership! God had matched them dollar for dollar! Now they could build the church, and today it stands as a witness to His promise, "In the hands of the Lord it will prove *more* than sufficient."

The Blight of Self-evaluation

If God so abundantly blesses every person and every company of believers, why are these instances so infrequent? Why do we not have new churches in every town and hamlet circling the globe? The answer is simply an unwillingness on our part to take Him at His word and a lack of faith to move forward. "Prove me now herewith," He invited through the prophet Malachi. But man, with his slide rules, calculators, and computers, measures his own potential and cautiously retreats into the dark cave of his own evaluations.

"Speak unto the children of Israel, that they go forward," God directed Moses (Ex. 14:15). Centuries later they were settled in ease and luxury, and God tried to stir them up again. "Enlarge the place of thy tent, and let them stretch forth the curtains of thine habitations: spare not, lengthen thy cords, and strengthen thy stakes. For thou shalt break forth on the right hand and on the left" (Isa. 54:2, 3).

Just consider the witness that God's people could bear if they would move out in faith. Miracle upon miracle would be wrought in their behalf and these would be a powerful witness to the truth and faith that they profess. "When the Lord gives a work to be done, let not men stop to inquire into the reasonableness of the command or the probable result of their efforts to obey."—*Ibid.*, p. 243. And possibly this is the answer to the problem, "men stop to inquire"!

The Unreasonableness of Faith

There are three rules for success in the work of God. First, one is to begin without any hesitation or question. Hesitancy cost Lot his wife. "If Lot himself had manifested no hesitancy to obey the angels' warning, but had earnestly fled toward the mountains, without one word of pleading or remonstrance, *his wife also would have made her escape.*"— *Patriarchs and Prophets,* p. 161. (Italics supplied.)

The moment a man hesitates to follow God's plans, the devil presents a host of reasons why it can't be done. One church down by the railroad tracks hesitated for years in an old dilapidated building because "everyone" knew they were too poor to build a church. If one of the members had placed in the building fund the money he must have spent for gasoline going from member to member convincing them that a new church was impossible, they would have had at least a beginning.

Then one day someone came out of his "cave" and saw that the world wasn't really dark at all—there was a sun in the sky. They began to "think rich." Now they could sing "I'm a Child of the King" without inserting the word "poor" before the word "child." They started to give. They worked with their hands. Soon the church was built and they moved in—not one whit poorer than when they were down by the tracks—in fact, they were more prosperous. And almost before the church was completed they began to plan for a gymnasium for their school (thinking rich does this to people). And they built it! It's amazing how much can be accomplished by God's firm when it is "God and Man, Unlimited"!

The second rule for success is that one must follow God's directions—specifically, without doubt or question. One may not always understand why, or how, or *if* it will work. Success is not dependent upon knowing why, but on doing.

> If perplexed, hold still; make no move in the dark.—*Testimonies,* vol. 5, p. 572.

> Often the Lord sees that His workers are in doubt as to what they should do. At such times, if they will put their confidence in Him, He will reveal to them His will.—*Ibid.,* vol. 9, p. 272.

The Bible records many instances of obedience and disobedience. The results never varied. Success always attended those who followed God's direction, failure those who disobeyed. There were two Sauls. One lost a kingdom because he wouldn't follow instructions; the other became the great apostle to the apostolic church because he in humility asked, *"Lord, what wilt thou have me to do?"* (Acts 9:6), and he did it. A man's potential is always dependent upon his willingness to follow God's instructions.

Third, one is not to be unduly concerned with the results.

> When we give ourselves wholly to God and in our work follow His directions, He makes Himself responsible for its accomplishment.—*Christ's Object Lessons,* p. 363.

Abraham tried to hurry God's schedule with a do-it-yourself plan. What a miserable failure that was. Rebekah never saw her favorite son, Jacob, after she tried to apply her own formula for success to God's plan.

What is a man's potential? It can only be measured by the yardstick of heaven. In the hands of God, a lowly fisherman becomes an evangelist and, with his friends, converts about three thousand in one day! A doctor, David Livingstone, who might have enjoyed his profession in the comfort of England, becomes a missionary and braves the jungles and fevers of Africa—and gives his life for the people he loves. What is a person's potential? It is unlimited in the hands of God.

15

WHAT IS SACRIFICE?

Sacrifice is the willingness to relinquish the entire life to God without any reservations.

As the skeptic so often asks, "What is truth?" so the Christian frequently wonders, "What is sacrifice?" This question has challenged both the scholar and the unlearned alike. One minister began his sermon with this statement, "I don't know what sacrifice is, and I don't think there is anyone in this congregation who knows."

In the vivid picture of the tempestuous times surrounding the second coming of Christ, His voice is heard instructing His angels, "Gather my saints together unto me; those that have made a covenant with me by sacrifice" (Ps. 50:5). It is only natural that those who want to be a part of this vast throng would have an earnest desire to know exactly what sacrifice really is.

Is Sacrifice Giving?

The term *sacrifice* is usually associated with the giving of money or material possessions. Frequently one hears of a person's "sacrificing" a piece of property for the church, or of making a "sacrificial" commitment. But does the giving of material things constitute sacrifice?

If one were to accept this interpretation, then a total sacrifice would be the giving of all one's possessions. This, however, would place a person in a strange position while still remaining in this world. His relationship to God as a manager would terminate, for he would have no possessions left to manage—and he would have nothing by which God could test either his capabilities or his attitude. All he could be expected to do would be to find some obscure corner in which to sit in idleness, for he would be altogether useless to himself and to those around him.

If sacrifice means the giving up of all earthly things, then Abraham, Jacob, Joseph, David, and Daniel certainly did not make a covenant with God by sacrifice, for they died very wealthy men. And still they were counted as worthy of eternal life.

Is Sacrifice Trading?

Webster has one thought-provoking definition of sacrifice: "A giving up of one thing for another." This concept has its proponents who urge men and women to trade the things of this world for eternal riches. This implies that a person could trade something he *owned* for something that God would give him in exchange.

But this assumption does not coincide with the Owner-manager principle at all. If a man is a manager and not an owner, what does he have to trade? Possessing nothing of his own, he is in a pretty poor position to do any bargaining.

For centuries men have been deluded with the idea that they could purchase salvation for themselves or their loved ones. But in order for a person to buy or trade, he would have to have complete control over some medium of exchange. Since God owns everything, the premise is incorrect that a man could buy or trade for anything of eternal value.

A Covenant by Sacrifice

The text (Ps. 50:5) does not say that those were to be gathered together who had *made a sacrifice*, but those who had *"made a covenant."* There are various ways to make a covenant, but in this case the covenant was made by sacrifice. How does one make a covenant by sacrifice? What is sacrifice? Note carefully how this covenant figured in the supreme test that came to Abraham.

If God had given him a choice—either all his possessions or his son—there can be no question as to what Abraham's decision would have been. He loved that boy more than everything he possessed. But God asked for the boy. After that agonizing trip to Mount Moriah, and the last-minute reprieve when the angel stayed his hand, God could say, "Now I know that thou fearest God, seeing thou hast not withheld thy son, thine only son from me" (Gen. 22:12). If sacrifice in this instance meant giving, he would have had to kill his son! But God accepted the fact that he had *not withheld* his son.

The patriarch had made a covenant with God a long time before in the land of Ur by placing himself completely in God's hands, willing to obey every command. This test proved more to Abraham than it did to God. God already knew he could stand the test. Now Abraham knew that his trust in God was not misplaced.

The Power of Choice

Although God owns the world and everything in it, there is one unique gift that God has given to man. This is the power of choice. This privilege was given to man at creation. The only thing that man can give God is his heart, as this represents his will. Solomon recognized this inalienable right of the individual when he said, "My son, give me thine heart" (Prov. 23:26). David understood the true meaning of sacrifice: "For thou desirest not sacrifice; else would I give it: thou delightest not in burnt offering. The *sacrifices of God* are a broken spirit: a broken and a contrite heart" (Ps. 51:16, 17).

In this context a person could make a covenant with God by the sacrifice of a broken spirit and a contrite heart. What is a man's "unbroken" spirit? It is the selfish desire and ambition of the carnal heart.

The sin that plagues every being and produces so many spiritual problems is selfishness. The natural heart eagerly seeks for self-gratification. It tries to obtain and keep to itself everything that will contribute to its own pleasure and security. The only aim of the human heart is *to get*. This is contrary to the principle of heaven, which is *to give*. The only way a person can make a covenant with God is by the complete sacrifice of the heart to His will.

Paul told of the terrible conflict that raged within him. "For the good that I would I do not: but the evil which I would not, that I do" (Rom. 7:19). His will and his desires were contrary to the will of God. Only by placing his life completely under God's control could he be safe. "I die daily," he wrote to the Corinthian believers (1 Cor. 15:31). After following this course of action to the close of his life he could say, "I have fought a good fight, I have finished my course, I have kept the faith" (2 Tim. 4:7). But this did not come by accident; Paul chose this course. On that memorable trip to Damascus he made his decision, "Lord, what wilt thou have me to do?" (Acts 9:6). He made his covenant with God by sacrificing his own will to that of God. This placed his life completely under God's control.

A Daily Covenant

The Lord requires us to be submissive to His will, subdued by His Spirit, and sanctified to His service. Selfishness must be put away, and we must overcome every defect in our characters as Christ overcame. In order to accomplish this work, we must die daily to self.—*Testimonies,* vol. 4, p. 66.

Right in the common walks of life is where self is to be denied and kept in subordination. . . . It is the daily dying to self in the little transactions of life that makes us overcomers.—*Ibid.,* vol. 2, p. 132.

This daily sacrifice of self will result in men and women becoming overcomers, and these will be the ones who will be gathered together unto Him. "To him that overcometh will I give to eat of the tree of life, which is in the midst of the paradise of God" (Rev. 2:7).

Sacrifice as It Applies to Management

Possibly the definition of sacrifice as the total relinquishing of every selfish trait and desire can be better understood from the viewpoint of *using* rather than *giving*. In this frame of reference the term will be compatible with both the distribution and continued possession of the Lord's goods. This would mean that the steward, or manager, would be continually receiving shipments of supplies from the great warehouses of heaven. He, as God's agent, would act as a distributor of these supplies to carry on the great work for the salvation of souls. As he is God's representative, every portion of his life would be under divine control.

This is compatible with the Owner-manager concept, in which everything that a man possesses is constantly available to the Owner whenever He requires it, and in whatever amount. All the selfish claims of the natural heart are relinquished. This is what is meant by placing everything on "the altar of sacrifice." The willingness to relinquish these claims constitutes sacrifice. This sacrifice fulfills the conditions of a covenant with God, and under these conditions a faithful manager can join the throng who have "made a covenant . . . by sacrifice."

16

PRINCIPLES OF PERSONAL FINANCE

The two great principles governing personal finance are responsibility and accountability.

There are those who believe that after the tithe and offerings have been set apart from their incomes, they are free to use the balance in any way they choose. In this they err. Everything belongs to God. All their time, talents, and means are His; they are only entrusted to them for their use. One is just as responsible for the last penny of his income as he is for the first. In the management of his life he must never forget that he is a manager—not an owner.

In every expenditure, every transaction, a person should ask, "Lord, what wilt thou have me to do?" This will put every decision under divine direction.

Divine Guidance Available

The management of life is subject to certain general principles that are spelled out in the manager's manual, the Bible. He also has other inspired instruction that amplifies these principles. In addition, he is promised the guidance of the Holy Spirit. "And thine ears shall hear a word behind thee, saying, This is the way, walk ye in it, when ye turn to the right hand, and when ye turn to the left" (Isa. 30:21). This leaves no excuse for the unwise management of personal finances.

Responsibility

Two great principles govern good, Christian management. The first is *responsibility*. This is a positive, present force that gives meaning and direction to the life. It gives any occupation or profession dignity, because the Christian manager is an agent of a firm whose Chairman of the board is God. The constant sense of responsibility will prevent rash decisions and costly mistakes. It will cause one to always seek for divine guidance and lessen his dependence upon human wisdom.

Accountability

The second great governing principle is *accountability*. The sense of responsibility will always be accompanied by a realization of accountability. In every activity there comes a time of reckoning, a time when the books are balanced. This is a personal accounting. "So then every one of us shall give account of himself to God" (Rom. 14:12). These two great principles, if fully realized, would answer most of life's perplexing problems. Very few mistakes would be made if they were the ruling force in every decision.

There are guidelines to personal finance that should be observed. Specific instruction has been given regarding these:

1. *Live within the income.* In a world in which the wants can so easily sway the reason, it is essential that the Christian manager exercise the greatest caution to avoid the pitfall of uncontrolled desire. "Be content with such things as ye have" (Heb. 13:5). "And having food and raiment let us be therewith content" (1 Tim. 6:8). Paul evidently overcame this same temptation, for he wrote, "I have learned, in whatsoever state I am, therewith to be content" (Phil. 4:11).

Whoever acquires more than sufficient for his real needs should seek wisdom and grace to know his own heart and to keep his heart diligently, lest he have imaginary wants and become an unfaithful steward, using with prodigality his Lord's entrusted capital.—*The Adventist Home,* p. 372.

2. *Practice economy.* If a person realizes that he is only an agent of the great firm of heaven, he will carefully control his finances, practicing economy in order that he may fully carry out his mission in life. To change the metaphor, as a soldier in the great army of God he will put everything he can into the "war effort" against evil. He will recognize that all the things of this world are to be classified into three divisions: essential, useful, and desirable. And he will keep these in their true perspective.

On the other hand, he will not go to the extreme on economy. Economy does not mean stinginess. He will neither be a spendthrift nor a miser. Many things are needed in the family for its comfort and convenience. These things should not be denied.

There are some who think that pure religion and prosperity do not go together. The heart can be just as pure in silk as in sackcloth. One cannot be any holier in a Volkswagen than in a Cadillac. Pure religion and rightdoing are associated not with poverty but with the wise management of entrusted goods under divine guidance.

Is it possible to go to the extreme on economy, giving more into the treasury of the Lord than is required? The answer is that it would be rare, but possible. One man was allowing his family to suffer for the necessities and some of the comforts of life because of his zeal for the Lord's work. His attention was called to this by God's servant.

In the home the same good principles of management must be employed that are essential in any business enterprise. Careful planning and budgeting will prove a safeguard to every family.

3. *Shun debt.* Learning to bind about the wants will prevent one of the most frequent of all family problems—financial perplexity. Through the medium of uncontrolled desire Satan binds men and women with the chains of debt that have proved to be the ruin of many families.

When one becomes involved in debt, he is in one of

Satan's nets, which he sets for souls. . . . Abstracting and using money for any purpose, before it is earned, is a snare.—*Ibid.*, p. 392.

Deny yourself a thousand things rather than run in debt. . . . Avoid it as you would the smallpox.—*Ibid.*, p. 393.

4. *Teach children how to handle money.* Children should be taught at an early age that all money comes from God, just like the ability to see, feel, and hear. They should be taught that money represents a portion of life, and is no more to be wasted than one would waste his own life. To throw money away is to throw life away!

They should be taught the tithing principle and the true reason for giving freewill offerings to God. The offerings that they give at church should not be doled out by their parents, but should come from money that they have earned or from their allowances. This will teach them responsibility to God. (See *The Adventist Home,* p. 387.)

Children should become acquainted with the costs of operating the home, the costs of clothing and education. They should be instructed to keep accurate accounts of their income and expenditures. Lessons of frugality will make them efficient men and women—faithful stewards of God.

5. *Save for a "rainy day."* Every family should have a reserve against emergencies that are to be expected in this life. There is a difference between saving for a "rainy day" and hoarding. This difference must be recognized. An emergency fund is just what the name implies—one that will tide the family over an unusual financial situation. Hoarding, on the other hand, stems from a belief that security depends on the accumulation of things. Whenever a person has enough goods laid by so he doesn't have to pray, "Give us this day our daily bread," he has too much.

This doesn't mean that one should live from hand to mouth, but it does mean that a daily dependence upon God is essential to both the temporal and the spiritual life.

Finally, God expects His people to live comfortably but not extravagantly. He expects them to regard themselves as temporary managers of temporary goods. He expects them to keep their eyes fixed on the real objective in life, which is a preparation for heaven and the new earth. He expects them to weigh the things of this world on the scales of heaven. He expects them to live in the world but not become a part of it.

The wise manager will recognize both his responsibility and accountability. With these clearly in mind, he will experience no difficulty in managing his personal finances.

17

PRINCIPLES OF CHURCH BUDGET FINANCE

If the faith of the members is not sufficient to impel them to adequately support the house of God, they should close it—He doesn't live there anymore!

One of the most important phases in the management of life is a person's wholehearted support of the church. God clearly showed His concern for this portion of a man's stewardship when He asked His people through the prophet Haggai, "Is it time for you, O ye, to dwell in your cieled houses, and this house lie waste?" (chap. 1:4). His blessing and their prosperity were dependent upon their making His house their first consideration.

The lack of temporal prosperity was the result of a neglect to put God's interests first.—*Prophets and Kings,* p. 573.

The financial perplexities that face most churches today are a dishonor to God. While a lack of adequate means is generally believed to be the church's greatest problem, this is not true. This lack is only a symptom—the real problem is selfishness.

God's Four-Point Plan

God certainly did not give His church a work to do on

earth and then leave it without sufficient funds to carry out its mission. In every plan that He has given to humanity there are four provisions that guarantee its fulfillment:

1. An exact, detailed blueprint.
2. The person or persons who are to carry it out.
3. The personal skills or talents required.
4. The necessary finances.

If the work be of God, He Himself will provide the means for its accomplishment.—*The Desire of Ages,* p. 371.

It must be obvious that if financial difficulties are being encountered in the work of the church either His plans are not being followed or the means that He has provided are being diverted into other channels. There are several factors that may contribute to this apparent problem.

Attitudes of the Members

There is a peculiar reasoning that many church members have in regard to church support. Because salvation is free, they appear to think that the church should operate without money. While accepting the fact that their own homes require constant care and maintenance, they ignore the same requirements in God's house.

This is substantiated by the small percentage of members who carry the major portion of the church budget load. This indifference is also shown in the attendance at the church business meetings. It would seem that if a person believed in something he would support it, not only by his means but by his presence and participation in its operation. But it is obvious that there are many church members who draw a distinction between their profession and their responsibility.

Lack of Involvement

Many people avoid becoming involved in anything that will cost them either time or money. One young man was urged by a friend to move from a large city church to a smaller one in the suburbs where he could become more deeply involved. He replied, "Where I go, I'm just a number. They don't know I exist—and that's the way I'm going to keep it."

Of what possible value could such a fringe membership be? Fire insurance? Why would he want to belong to any organization without becoming involved?

As strange as it may seem, the church is to some extent, at least, responsible for some of the attitudes of its members. Some of its approaches for financial support have certainly not been conducive to the development of responsible Christian stewardship.

Popular Appeals for Funds

Apologetic approach: The needs of the church are sometimes given the flavor of a "necessary evil." Giving is portrayed as a painful experience. On occasion one hears the jest, "The tenderest nerve in the body is the one that goes from the pocketbook to the brain!"

Any reference to giving should never be made the subject of a joke. Giving, in God's sight, is a sacred evidence of love and devotion—any other kind is mockery.

It were better not to give at all than to give grudgingly; for if we impart of our means when we have not the spirit to give freely, *we mock God.—Counsels on Stewardship,* p. 199. (Italics supplied.)

Offering plate approach: Many churches conduct their financial programs in a slipshod, hand-to-mouth manner. Their needs are always presented as individual emergencies. The offering (or collection) plate goes round and round. This multiplicity of appeals gives the church a commercial atmosphere, or places it in the role of a beggar.

In the operation of a home, the income, representing a single sum, is distributed to cover the many operating expenses. The financial requirements of a church should likewise be supplied from one general fund. Such is the case when a church operates on a planned church budget.

Juvenile approach: Many times juvenile methods are used to stimulate adult participation. In one church, each member who had reached a particular goal for some current project was permitted to walk to the front and place a plastic bee on a styrofoam hive! This might be suitable for children—but for adults? One must question the maturity of a membership that requires some of the goal charts that are used to stimulate it into action.

Substitute approach: It is difficult to understand the reasoning behind the suggestions for substitutes for personal sacrifice when they are so contrary to Christian belief and teaching.

One pastor, who said he had been doing some thinking (?), told his members that if each of them "tipped" the Lord five cents for each meal, in three years they could raise forty-three thousand dollars—*and not know they'd given anything!* Did he consider God a waiter to be tipped?

The following definition of Investment was heard in another church: "Investment is a project that we use to get money for new work, *so we don't have to dig down in our own pockets and get it!*"

The selfish heart will gleefully embrace any method that will permit its owner to retain that which he considers his. The church that encourages this approach to financial support is planting the seeds of its own spiritual destruction.

There Is No Shortage of Funds

God has placed sufficient means in the hands of His people to amply sustain His work. There is no reason for any other approach than the responsibility of those who love Him and His work.

A valuable lesson regarding the support of God's house can be learned from the instruction given to the Israelites. The giver was to place his offerings and first fruits in a basket and bring them to the Temple. The priest took the basket and placed it before the altar of the Lord. The donor was then required to make a public statement. He began by saying, "A Syrian ready to perish was my father, and he went down into Egypt . . ." (Deut. 26:5).

Then he gave a brief history of God's deliverance from the land of captivity and the journey to the Promised Land. He vowed that he had taken all the hallowed things out of his house, and had kept the commandments of God. He concluded this recital with this prayer, "Look down from thy holy habitation, from heaven, and bless thy people Israel, and the land which thou hast given us, as thou swarest unto our fathers, a land that floweth with milk and honey" (verse 15).

How His Gifts Were Used

These freewill offerings were placed in the treasury of the Temple for its upkeep and service. The point to be remembered is that the giver did not give to any specific operating expenses associated with the maintenance of the Temple. He gave to God—not to things. His gifts were the outflowing of a heart filled with love and gratitude for the blessings he had received.

If people would follow this plan today in giving to God instead of to things, all the needs of the church would be constantly supplied. It is the selfish withholding of the means which God has provided that is responsible for its financial problems.

Responsibility of Leadership

No discussion of church finance would be complete without calling attention to the responsibility of leadership to properly manage the means entrusted to it. This is a stewardship of the greatest importance, for not only are these people responsible to God for the means given for His work, but they are also responsible for maintaining the trust and confidence that these monies reflect.

Sometimes there has been an attitude on the part of leadership that once a person places his offering in the treasury, he shouldn't question its management or use. This is irresponsible thinking. While a person should be disinterested in his benevolence (not allowing his emotions to govern his giving), he must be encouraged to maintain a high degree of interest in the objects for which the funds are used. His cooperation and confidence in administration will be in direct proportion to the openness of the communication that is maintained in this area.

A church cannot operate any more efficiently on an offering-plate routine than could a business enterprise. Therefore, each church should carefully plan its yearly program in advance. This should be an accurate, workable estimate based on its financial potential as indicated by the annual tithe. Everything should be done to involve as many of the members as possible in both the planning and funding of this budget.

The Church Budget

Without question the very best plan for financing the activities of the church is to combine all the maintenance and expansion plans into a church budget. This will free the worship service from the repeated calls for money. It will also allocate to each department the amount of means needed for its efficient operation. *It will control spending.*

This plan provides the member with an easily understood way to support the total program of the church without having to determine how much to give to which fund. He simply gives one amount (to local work) each week, or month, and this is distributed to the various needs by the church treasurer in accordance with the budget adopted by the church in business session.

The Finance Committee

All the business of the church should be conducted by a finance committee. This committee should be chosen by the church during the regular election of officers. The pastor and the church treasurer are always ex officio members.

The duties of this committee are to (1) prepare the budget, (2) implement its financing, and (3) manage the budget in accordance with its approval by the church.

It is unfortunate that many members are not interested enough in the operation of the church to attend the business meetings. Every effort must be extended to make it impossible for them to misunderstand the operation of the church.

Preparing the Budget

The budget may be planned for the calendar or the fiscal year. Many churches find that the crowded program at the year's end makes the fiscal year a better plan.

1. The finance committee secures from each department head (Sabbath school superintendent, head elder, head deacon, chairman of the school board, Dorcas leader, lay activities leader, et cetera) a detailed list of the anticipated needs and budget for the ensuing year. This information is compiled into a suggested budget, using the annual tithe as a basis for potential control. (A church's potential for local operation, including the church school subsidy, is usually limited to an amount equal to 50 to 60 percent of its annual tithe.)

2. The proposed budget is submitted by the finance committee chairman to the church board for approval. It may be accepted, changed, or adjusted at this time.

3. The church, in business session, studies, adjusts if necessary, and approves the budget.

4. Once each month a brief statement should be placed in the church bulletin (perhaps in an insert) showing the total amount of income and expenditures for the month.

5. The church treasurer should refer any financial problems to the chairman of the finance committee, not to the pastor. All announcements regarding the finances of the church should be made by this chairman or other authorized layman. This will relieve the pastor of the stigma of a fund raiser, with which he is too often associated.

Keeping the Machinery Oiled and in Operation

Most Christians have been educated to give to appeals. Planned giving (a requirement for a successful church budget program) will require an extensive and continuous reeducation in the true principles of giving. This may be accomplished in three ways:

Involvement: Try to get as many of the members as possible involved in the church budget plan. Home-to-home visitation has proved a valuable aid. These must be spiritual visits calling attention to the blessings that attend compliance with God's requirements. *Don't go fund raising!*

The visitor explains the budget, answers any questions, and invites participation. *He does not ask about, nor take, a commitment.* This is a sacred area between the member and God—the visitor must not trespass here. Now the member is free to make and turn in his own commitment.

Communication: Make it impossible for every member *not to know* about every activity of the church. Regular reports should be rendered regarding the progress of any projects involved and the financial status of the church operation. This can be accomplished through the church bulletins, bulletin inserts, or letters from the pastor or finance committee chairman. *Be sure that everybody knows!*

Education: To a large extent this is the pastor's part in the plan. God's great principles of life management should be woven into sermons, studied at prayer meetings, and emphasized during offertory time. Personal testimonies from time to time are of inestimable value. *This is God's plan—tell about it!*

Caution: You Can Kill a Church Budget Plan

By failure to observe the following points, you can destroy the value of a budget.

1. *Don't tamper with it.* After the budget has been approved by the church in business session, it must not be changed to suit the whim of some individual. If properly prepared it will need no adjustment. If a major change becomes necessary, this must be done with the full approval of the church in another business session. *Don't tamper with it!*

2. *Follow the plan.* If a large percentage of the church persists in giving to specific projects, according to their individual preferences, the church budget plan will prove ineffective. A cooperative effort by a majority of the membership is essential.

3. *Don't add on some additional projects.* All the projects in which the church wishes to engage during the year must be included in the church budget. To attempt to add side projects will destroy any budget plan (in home or church).

The evils of multiple promotions and appeals that the church budget is designed to eliminate, can be nullified by untimely ideas.

Support It or Close It

An experience may serve to illustrate this seemingly strange advice. One church, which had followed the rules for a carefully prepared budget, found itself in difficulty because the receipts each month failed to cover the budget by nearly one hundred dollars.

They had several choices. They could harp on the deficit during the church services—and pass the plate! They could resort to some fund-raising gimmick. They could reduce their budget to match the income.

The church was called together for a business meeting. The budget was placed on the blackboard and the problem explained. It was suggested that certain items could be eliminated in order to bring it into balance.

One brother rose to his feet and said, "But, you can't do that!" He was reminded that it is impossible to pay bills without money. There was silence for a time, then the same man arose with another suggestion.

"I don't like the idea of eliminating anything. I have a better plan. Why don't we each give more?"

This suggestion was unanimously adopted. The treasurer stated later that for the first time in the history of the church there is now a surplus in the treasury.

The Adult Approach

Church support is an adult problem and should be considered from an adult viewpoint. But it would be no problem if each member felt as David did when he said, "I was glad when they said unto me, Let us go into the house of the Lord" (Ps. 122:1).

The maintenance of God's house should be conducted with a proper regard for its importance in the management of life. The church and its welfare should be a member's first consideration, *for it is God's house.*

18

THE CHURCH BUILDING PROGRAM

If a congregation has to have a fund-raising compaign before they can build a church, they're not ready to build a house for God.

If one were to ask a small child, "What is a church?" he might get an old rhyme and a finger play for an answer:

> Here is a church,
> This is the steeple,
> Open the door—
> And see all the people!

And strange as it may seem, some adult views haven't progressed far beyond this childish understanding, for to many of them the church either has never been, or has lost its original purpose as being, God's house.

Somehow in today's sophisticated atmosphere, the church isn't generally regarded with the same awe and reverence as was held by a perhaps more primitive society. This fact was brought out by a man who had visited one of the islands of the South Seas. He told of a church that consisted of a pole structure with a thatched roof. There were no side walls, but there was a wall in the front, with a door. When the people came to church early, they waited outside until someone unlocked the door! Although they might have entered from either side, they didn't because of the reverence they had for this house of God.

It is a tragic mistake for anyone to fail to recognize the lofty character of a dwelling dedicated to the worship of God. But possibly this is the reason for the gross irreverence seen in many churches. It may also account for the evident reluctance of many congregations to provide generously for the building and maintenance of a church. What greater thing could a person do than to construct and care for an abode where God has promised to dwell if only "two or three are gathered together in my name" (Matt. 18:20)?

Is the Church God's House?

Before entering into any discussion about the building of a church, the premise must be established that not every church building is a house of God. The two are not synonymous. Bricks and mortar, steeple and pews do not determine whether a building is a house of God.

Certainly He will not dwell where there is disunity and strife. Neither will He be found where pride and selfishness are manifested. Therefore, the style and architecture of a building do not determine if it is a house of God. Rather, it is the spirit of the people inside. They *are* the church. Their faith and consecration make the difference. So in preparing to build a church, first consideration must be given to the membership and its relationship to God.

Requisites for Building a Church

Almost without exception, the requisites that are considered in a church building program are (1) plans, (2) site, and (3) money. But there are other requisites that are rarely considered. Without them the edifice may have the appearance of a church, but it will never fulfill the requirements for a house of God.

These requisites were brought to view in the experience of the Israelites when they were instructed to build a sanctuary in the wilderness. Moses was given plans covering every detail for this magnificent structure. Everything was ready—but before construction was begun they turned away from God and became involved with a calf that Aaron said jumped out of a bonfire when he threw in all their golden earrings! God told them they couldn't build Him a house—not under these circumstances. Plans, site, and materials—all ready—but they couldn't build!

By their apostasy the Israelites forfeited the blessing of divine Presence, and for a time rendered impossible the erection of a sanctuary for God among them. But after they were again *taken into favor with Heaven,* the great leader proceeded to execute the divine command.—*Patriarchs and Prophets,* p. 343. (Italics supplied.)

How many congregations today spend any time considering whether they are in divine favor before planning a house for God? They are usually so engrossed in site, plans, and money that they give little, if any, thought to this essential condition. Is it any wonder that sometimes it takes years to heal the division that often results from a church building program?

One head elder said it had taken twelve years for the wounds from their church building program to heal sufficiently so the members could work together again. Twelve wasted years!

Note carefully the first requisites for preparing a house for God:

Devotion to God and a *spirit of sacrifice* were the *first requisites* in preparing a dwelling place for the Most High.—*Ibid.* (Italics supplied.)

These two divinely prescribed requisites would eliminate the problems associated with church building programs. *Devotion to God* would provide all the time, energy, and finances needed for the building. A *spirit of sacrifice* would permit a harmonious adjustment of personal likes and dislikes.

These characteristics among the members would generate a spirit of unity that is essential to the success of every endeavor. This spirit of unity would provide ample space for the ideas of others and a willingness to cooperate with the majority decisions of the church.

They should also feel it a solemn duty to illustrate in their characters the teachings of Christ, being at peace one with another and moving in perfect harmony as an undivided whole. They should *defer their individual judgment* to the judgment of the body of the church.—*Testimonies,* vol. 4, p. 18. (Italics supplied.)

Such a condition in the church would make it possible for *divine power to combine with human effort.* This is the only condition under which a building can become a house of God—not just a church.

Building the Church

There are some special instructions that should be considered when contemplating the building of a house of God. If these are followed, many problems can be averted.

1. *Planning must be a group effort.* Great care should be exercised to ensure the democratic process of voice and representation in all decisions regarding the church building program. However, it is equally important that the members *"defer their individual judgment to the judgment of the body of the church."* Never should one person or one group of people seek to dominate.

One man's mind and judgment is not to be allowed to become an efficiency in any case where the building of a church is concerned. . . . This is a lesson you must learn, to seek the mind and judgment of your brethren, and not advance without their advice, counsel, and cooperation.—*Counsels on Stewardship,* p. 262.

2. Consider the needs of other churches. In all planning for local work or buildings, the needs of other areas should be kept in mind. The church must remember that it is a part of a greater body, and the welfare of this larger group is dependent upon a balanced work in every place.

Therefore, in every plan this wider area of responsibility must be kept in mind. This would prevent the extravagant overbuild that results in magnificent structures in a few places while other communions are forced by their size and potential to limp along with inadequate facilities.

When plans are laid to erect a building in one place, give careful consideration to other places that are in just as great need of money for the erection of needful buildings.—*Testimonies,* vol. 7, p. 284.

The Building

3. Do not be extravagant. There is a danger in building a church that is similar to the building of a home—the "wants" tend to override the "needs." It is so easy to add a little here and a little there. Each item seems to add such a small amount to the overall cost. But when these are all added together, they add up to a substantial sum.

Take care in the matter of ornamentation in the building of a house for God. Plain beauty, order, and taste should characterize it.

God would not have His people expend means extravagantly for show or ornament, but He would have them observe neatness, order, taste, and plain beauty in preparing a house for Him in which He is to meet with His people.—*Ibid.,* p. 257.

In its design, the church building is to be in "accordance with His character and majesty" (*ibid.,* vol. 5, p. 268). If the planners had kept this in mind, it is doubtful that one would see some of the strange buildings that are constructed for His worship.

Good taste would indicate that a church should fit into the location in which it is built. This may call for different styles of architecture in different places.

Churches are built in many places, but they need not all be built in precisely the same style. Different styles of building may be appropriate to different locations.—*Evangelism,* p. 379.

4. Use good materials and build well. In both the building of the tabernacle and the Temple only the best materials and workmanship were employed. Every sacrifice and offering made to God was to be perfect. This same principle must be followed in the construction of a church. Never must it be thought that because this world is soon to be destroyed, the church can be of poor construction. This

is God's house and must be regarded as such.

Would we dare to dedicate to God a house made of cheap material, and put together so faultily as to be almost lifted from its foundations when struck by a strong wind? . . . Whatever you do, let it be done as well as upright principles and your strength and skill can do it.—*Ibid.*, p. 378.

A word of caution:

It is when the character building is neglected, when the adornment of the soul is lacking, when the simplicity of godliness is lost sight of, that pride and love of display demand magnificent church edifices, splendid adornings, and imposing ceremonials.—*Christ's Object Lessons*, p. 298.

The Site

A person building a house for himself usually builds it where he wishes to live. This same principle should be applied when building a house for God. Too often God is not consulted in this matter. Those planning to build a church are influenced by their personal preferences.

One church, which was experiencing difficulty in finding a suitable building site, was asked if they had consulted God about the problem. They admitted that they had not.

The church was called together for a special meeting and almost the entire congregation was present. First, they asked God *if* He would allow them to build a house for Him. Then they asked Him *where* He wanted His house built. Realizing that their first petition depended upon their devotion to God and a spirit of sacrifice, they united in a reconsecration of themselves to Him. They recognized that they would have to wait for His answer to their second request.

A few days following this meeting, the pastor was impressed to drive to a certain section of the city where there was a small acreage that would be an excellent site for the church. Although he had been told by a number of realtors that this property could not be purchased (each of them had tried separately to buy it) he was directed to the owner's home.

To the kind woman who came to the door he explained that he was the pastor of the Seventh-day Adventist church. Then he inquired if there was any possibility that she might consider selling the land in question for a church site. She smiled and said she would be delighted to have a Seventh-day Adventist church built there.

So often in the conduct of God's work it is forgotten that consecrated human effort must be combined with divine power, human knowledge with divine wisdom, human ideas with divine planning. God knows the exact location on which His houses are to be constructed—one has only to ask.

The Funds for His House

God has placed means in the hands of His people with which to accomplish His work. No program will be successful unless the members contemplating the building of a church are willing to give to the limit of their ability. It is not until they reach this limit that God can work in their behalf, because if they do not give to the limit of their capacity they show a spirit of selfishness. A *spirit of sacrifice* is one of the first requisites for preparing a dwelling place for the Most High.

He has provided His people with a surplus of means, that when He calls for help, they may cheerfully respond.—*Counsels on Stewardship,* p. 45.
Everyone can give something.

He calls for offerings from those who can give, and even the poorer members can do their little. And when there is a will to do, God will open the way.—*Ibid.,* p. 263.

The *small sums* saved by deeds of sacrifice will do more for the upbuilding of the cause of God than larger gifts will accomplish that have not called for denial of self.—*Testimonies,* vol. 9, pp. 157, 158. (Italics supplied.)
Offerings must be given willingly.

It were *better not to give at all* than to give grudgingly;

for if we impart of our means when we have not the spirit to give freely, we mock God.—*Counsels on Stewardship,* p. 199. (Italics supplied.)
Give your best offering.

If you build a house for the Lord, do not offend and limit Him by casting in your lame offerings. *Put the very best offering* into a house built for God.—*Testimonies,* vol. 1, p. 196. (Italics supplied.)
Use money wisely.

It is His plan that the means which He has entrusted to them be used judiciously.—*Ibid.,* p. 197.
Beware the borrowed dollar.

In some cases it may be better to hire some money than not to build.—*Gospel Workers,* p. 432.

Every debt upon every house of worship among us may be paid if the members of the church will plan wisely and put forth earnest, zealous effort to cancel the debt.—*Ibid.,* p. 434.

While you have thought much of your own selves, of your own selfish interests, you have either neglected to arise and build, or have built on hired money, and have not made donations to free the church buildings of debt. ... *The interest swallows up the means* that should be used to pay off the principle.—*Counsels on Stewardship,* p. 261. (Italics supplied.)

Things to Avoid

1. The overbuild: There are churches today that are heavily burdened with debt because restraint was not exercised in their building plans. While every church should plan for some extension, there is a point beyond which it would be better to "swarm." A church that becomes too large provides a climate for anonymity. This makes it easy to avoid involvement. God warns against "Jerusalem centers."

2. The remaining debt: What could be more discouraging to a membership than a large debt after the building is completed? Money that should be reducing the principle is swallowed up by interest. A good plan is to get as

much money as possible in hand *before* starting construction. It would be better to postpone the start of a building project than to build prematurely and experience the throes of trying to pay off a large loan.

It is dishonoring to God for our churches to be burdened with debt. This state of things need not exist. It shows wrong management from beginning to end, and it is a dishonor to the God of heaven.—*Ibid.*, p. 261.

The Need for Anticipated Income

Those who build a house of God are to give so willingly that the workmen are forced to say, "Bring no more" (see *Patriarchs and Prophets,* pp. 346, 347). There will be times, however, when income must be anticipated in order to begin preliminary work on the project. Otherwise the church may have to wait until all the funds are in hand. The same principle is involved whenever a driver pulls into a service station for gas. He has to know whether to say, "Put in a gallon" or "Fill 'er up."

My experience has been that sometimes a fund-raising campaign has met this need for information by using social and financial pressures to get members to sign a pledge, commitment, or covenant. But a procedure has been found that satisfies the need for information and commitment without violating the principle of allowing each individual to give *"as he purposeth in his heart."* This is called the "unsigned commitment."

Each member is visited *in his home.* (The visitor can be anyone as long as he or she *believes* in the work of the church and is an active participant in it.) The purpose of the visit is threefold: (1) to explain the program, (2) to explain the need for establishing a *rate of income,* (3) to give an invitation to participate.

Sample approach:

"I have called to discuss with you our proposed budget for the coming year. [This approach works equally well with a new building program.] As we go over these items I hope you will feel free to discuss them and ask questions.

"Before any project can be accomplished, a source, or

rate of income, must be established. This is true in the home budget as well as in the church. After this rate of income is known, your church board (or building committee) can proceed with their plans.

"To establish this rate of income, we are asking each member to prayerfully consider his *proportionate* share in the project (what he might be able to do on a systematic basis under God's blessing), and indicate this decision on this anonymous commitment card. You may place this card in the offering plate next Sabbath.

"These amounts (weekly, monthly, or other designated time) will be combined into a monthly rate of income, which will permit the church board (or building committee) to function intelligently and efficiently.

"I'm sure you agree with me that each of us bears a responsibility not only to the group but, more important, to God, and if each of us does his part the burden will rest lightly but with due weight on all. I am not asking for, nor do I wish to take, your commitment—or know what it is to be. This is a sacred area between you and God. I am asking that you, as a fellow member, help us in carrying on the Lord's work. (The visitor closes the interview with prayer.)

The Divine Ingredient

Every congregation must realize it is impossible for them to build a house for God. "Except the Lord build the house, they labour in vain that build it" (Ps. 127:1). They must realize that God is the Builder—they are only the helpers. With this realization, all the problems usually associated with building programs will disappear, for in God's sight there are no difficulties—He has no limitations.

They must never lose sight of the fact that the requisites for building a house of God are, first, devotion to God and, second, a spirit of sacrifice. When these conditions are met God makes Himself responsible for the success of the project.

19

COLLECTIVE SELFISHNESS

The selfishness of a group is the perfect media in which individual selfishness will flourish.

Collective selfishness refers to the attitudes and practices of a group that desires to spend all its resources either on or within its own body. This syndrome is usually seen in the reluctance of one church to assist in some project in which a number of churches, or the conference, is involved.

No Church Is an Island

It has been said that "no man is an island." This is equally true of a church. A church cannot isolate itself from a group bound together by a common belief and having a mutual purpose without definite self-damage. Scattered across the country are many little churches that once belonged to a central organization, but that have for some reason withdrawn to themselves. Not one of these has conducted, or would be able to conduct, a worldwide program. Most of them face a continual struggle to stay alive, and many of them have been forced to close their doors for lack of support.

Collective selfishness, as currently seen, is usually the

result of an idea that a church has all it can do just to take care of its own financial problems without being concerned about those of others. This is especially true where church and school budgets are unusually large.

However, this idea, if put into action, will only compound its problems. This is group selfishness and provides the perfect media in which individual selfishness will grow. Ellen White wrote, "The law of self-serving is the law of self-destruction."—*The Desire of Ages,* p. 624.

The Group Relationship

There is an interesting analogy that exists between the inner-church relationship and the church-group relationship. After a new member is baptized he should be drawn into the fellowship of the church for his own strength and protection. Enfolded within the varying strengths of the other members, he is protected, to some extent at least, from outside influences. As he engages in and supports the various activities of the church, the new member becomes welded to the membership and he eventually blends into its body.

Solomon endorsed group effort in these words: "Two are better than one; because they have a good reward for their labour. For if they fall, the one will lift up his fellow: but woe to him that is alone when he falleth; for he hath not another to help him up" (Eccl. 4:9, 10).

Likewise, a church must be protected by the church-group relationship. This group is bound together by the adhesive of similar beliefs, aims, and objectives. In this relationship, the larger churches can be a strength to the smaller ones. Objectives that would be impossible or impractical for one church are well within the capabilities of many churches working together. In such an association, the individual church holds the same position to the corporate body as its members have to its own communion. As it expects responsibility and cooperation from its members, so it must assume responsibility and cooperation to the group of churches to which it belongs.

If a church shirks or refuses to carry out its church-group obligation, it sets a dangerous precedent. By shunning its responsibility it gives license to each of its own members to also shun his responsibility, for it has established an inner-group precedent. Once this pattern has been set it can no longer expect responsible support and cooperation for its own operation. One illustration will suffice:

A certain church promised to contribute a specified sum to a church-group project. They never fulfilled this promise. After years of financial problems, they promised to make good on this original commitment and to give a certain percentage of their income to a new project.

For a few months they fulfilled these promises and for the first time in years received sufficient funds to adequately care for their own church and school needs. Then, in studying the church budget one evening in board meeting, someone called attention to the sum of money they were contributing to the church-group project and questioned the wisdom of sending all this money out of the local church. Collective selfishness grows in any kind of soil, and a motion was soon made to cut the appropriation to less than half. The strange thing about it is that they didn't cut it in half—they just cut it out! Within a very short time they were in financial difficulty again.

Such is the effect of collective selfishness on the motivation of the local membership. It is a self-destructive force, and many churches today find themselves in a constant financial struggle without realizing that they have, by their own actions, created this problem.

Group Effort

The worldwide program, with its publishing houses, schools, hospitals, and mission stations, has been the result of a combined effort by many people. Not only is the gospel commission dependent upon the unified action of every believer, but the individual church must be an active member of this organization if it is to grow numerically and spiritually.

For this reason, churches are united into conferences,

conferences into unions, unions into divisions, and divisions into a world organization. A church pulling away from the organization will not destroy the organization any more than a small limb cut from a large tree will destroy the tree. It is always the limb that dies—not the tree. The church that detaches itself, even in attitude, from the sisterhood of churches to which it belongs will die spiritually, though its doors may remain open for services.

This spirit of *unsectional liberality* should characterize the churches of today. They should continually keep the burden on their souls for the advancement of the cause of God *in any and every place.* Benevolence is the very foundation of the universe.—*Sketches From the Life of Paul,* p. 175. (Italics supplied.)

Concern for Others

This spirit of genuine concern for others must motivate every believer, every church, for this is the spirit of Christ. A church must always look beyond itself if its vision is to remain bright. It must not make comparisons within its own body, for these restrict the vision. Paul said, "They measuring themselves by themselves, and comparing themselves among themselves, are not wise" (2 Cor. 10:12).

It must never seek money only for itself, but for others, as well. And as the collective spirit of unselfishness is demonstrated in its concern and regard for other people, other churches, and other fields, a church will find that resources sufficient for its own requirements will constantly flow into its treasury. The spirit of unselfishness that will characterize its actions will be a perfect media in which its members can develop unselfish characters.

20

A CANDID LOOK AT CHURCH FUND RAISING

In the area of finance, the church faces one of her most vulnerable points.

In probably no other area has the church committed or suffered so many abuses as in the field of finance. In its constant search for funds to carry on its functions it has often lost much of its influence and missionary zeal. During the long ages of compulsory support it became a cruel master rather than a kindly shepherd. In the subsequent period of voluntary giving (so called) it has become, in the minds of many of its members, a beggar rather than a crusader against evil.

The reason for this dilemma is that the church has failed to accept and carry out the only plan for its financial support that God ordained. Behind the scene has been Satan's plan to blot out the truth of God's absolute ownership. Working through selfish, human instrumentalities, he has instituted plans that have caused disappointment and confusion in the minds of many believers, and limited the work of the church. Instead of using its time and energies in carrying out its divine commission, it has wasted these vital forces in its efforts to survive.

Primary Purpose Lost

A frightening thought evolves from a study of church finance. As money making becomes necessary, the spiritual leaders tend to lose sight of the primary purpose of the church. The progress of the church is then measured by the success or failure of its fund-raising campaigns. The spiritual needs of its members are often neglected because of the pressures of financial goal reaching. Even the cost of winning a soul has been evaluated in money! But the possession of wealth by a church has never proved to be a blessing. The church has always made its greatest spiritual growth under apparent adversity—with a shortage of visible resources but with an abundance of faith and zeal.

A Study of Church Fund Raising

Because so many methods of church fund raising are in vogue today, it is essential that they be considered carefully in order to determine whether they are compatible with God's plan for financing His work.

In the time of Israel, God's method for the support of the Temple and the care of the poor was by the use of the means given to Him in the tithes and offerings. His plan was simple and equitable. It placed the responsibility proportionately but lightly on every person. However, by the time of Christ the church leaders, in their desire to enrich themselves, had laid down a multitude of exacting rules governing these instructions. The great principles underlying them were obliterated, as were the lessons they were designed to teach.

Jesus exposed one of their fraudulent practices when He cried, "Woe unto you, scribes and Pharisees, hypocrites! for ye devour widows' houses" (Matt. 23:14). He was exposing their plot in persuading widows to donate their property to the Temple, then using it to their own selfish advantage. Is it possible that we may face the same dangers today?

From the exactions of the law, church support in the apostate Christian church moved even a step lower—into compulsory giving. Tithes and gifts were demanded under pain of excommunication. For centuries the grinding heel of church oppression was felt.

While the Reformation freed many people from some of the religious abuses of the time, it did not wholly release them from the church's financial oppression. Somehow these godly men never really understood in their fullness all the great truths that they taught. It seems incredible that they could teach that salvation was free and still fail to understand that God also accepts only freewill offerings and willing service.

Even many of those who fled the tithe-tax system in England brought compulsory church support to America, where it was in many places rigorously enforced. Men were fined for nonattendance at church and for other reasons. A man who failed to pay his church assessments was liable to the confiscation of his livestock or farm implements to satisfy the debt.

When public resentment made this type of support no longer possible, other means had to be sought if the church was to survive. These included pew-rent plans, lotteries, and bazaars, to name a few. None of these methods provided sufficient funds to allow the church to adequately carry out her divine mission, simply because they were the plans of men, not those of God.

The Every-Member Canvass

Of all the plans and methods devised, the most financially successful was the traditional pressure-oriented every-member canvass. This was a carefully orchestrated procedure in which every member of the church was solicited for a predetermined amount or pledge to finance the church program. Different types of pressure were brought to bear on the member. The method proved to be more successful for raising money for new church buildings than for budget programs, but even in these it enjoyed a degree of success. Generally speaking, large sums of money were pledged and often paid. Churches and schools stand today as silent, positive witnesses to the success of many of these campaigns.

But there is also a not-so-silent minority who bear an entirely negative testimony to the pressures that were built into the canvass structure. And there is a very vocal majority who, having once participated in such a program, say, "Never again!"

Results Not Always as Advertised

Attention must be directed to the fact that the results of these programs were usually measured by commitments—not actual money. Often these commitments were not paid within the three-year period that was the normal life of the program. This, of course, removes much of the glamour of the "instant money" image. It is almost like the man who said he was a millionaire because he was making a dollar a day—one million days, one million dollars! In some conference expansion programs, where the commitment totals were loudly acclaimed at the close of the solicitation period, only about forty-seven percent of the money committed actually came into the treasury!

However, regardless of the apparent success or failure of this program, something is lacking in the spirituality of the church when the faith that it professes does not motivate its members to give without having their benevolent impulses stimulated by the so-called dynamics of fund raising. If a person has to be coerced into giving, he shouldn't give, for his offering wouldn't be accepted by the Lord anyway.

The Dynamics of Pressure-Oriented Programs

What is the inherent factor in the traditional, pressure-oriented, every-member-canvass program that places it in opposition to God's plan? It is the pressure that forms the basis for every procedure. God gave man the freedom of choice, and this should never be violated, regardless of the merit of the objective or the urgency of the need. The end does not justify the means. The canvass program was based on social pressure—the influence-pressure factor that one individual has upon another. Note carefully how some of these pressures were subtly applied:

Guilt: The dynamics of the canvass program were based on some questionable psychological procedures. First, there was the guilt feeling that consciously or subconsciously pervaded the membership. This feeling came from the fact that they were compelled to hire professional fund raisers from outside their church because of their unwillingness to give freely. It was a secret recognition of their own selfishness. This at least produced a degree of willingness to "go along" with whatever plan was presented.

Catalyst: Second was the injection of the catalyst, which was the hired canvass director. This person, with a forceful personality and a carefully planned and directed program, exerted a tremendous influence on the membership—at least temporarily.

Social pressure: Third was the factor of influence, which in this case was the financial-social influence or pressure. Influence, like water, flows downhill. This principle, as applied in fund raising, simply meant that a person could influence to make "sacrificial" gifts only those with income potentials equal to or below his own level. This social pressure is one of the greatest motivating forces in human relations.

In every major fund-raising drive, such as the United Way, Heart Fund, et cetera, the person chosen to head the program is always one of the top financial leaders of the community. This is done primarily for the influence he can exert over other financial leaders (and with the anticipation that he will contribute about 10 percent of the total objective!).

In church fund raising, such a "top-dollar man" was also sought to serve as the general chairman. The means often used to get such a person to accept this position were in themselves ingenious. With the enlistment of this financial leader began the recruitment of other financially influential persons. This eventually formed a pyramid of social-influence pressure down through the membership to the one with the very least giving ability. Each of these people exerted this social-influence pressure on those equal to or directly beneath his level of financial potential.

Sacrificial influence: It is strange that this "top-dollar" influence should be used in the church when Jesus held up the example of the poor widow and her sacrificial gift as the influence factor for all Christians to emulate. Paul cited the church at Philippi as a worthy example: "How that in a great trial of affliction the abundance of their joy and their deep poverty abounded into the riches of their liberality. For to their power, I bear record, yea, and beyond their power they were willing of themselves, praying with much intreaty that we would receive the gift" (2 Cor. 8:2-4).

The experience of the Israelites during the time when David was preparing materials for the Temple has been used as a Biblical basis for these traditional pressure-oriented canvass programs. But is this reasonable? According to the records the people were influenced by several factors: (1) David's testimony of his own heart's desire: "I have prepared with all my might for the house of my God" (1 Chron. 29:2); (2) the enormous size of his gifts; and (3) the willing offerings of their chiefs and rulers.

But the people's willing and spontaneous response came when David challenged them, "And who then is willing to consecrate his service this day unto the Lord?" (verse 5). "Then the people rejoiced, for that they offered willingly, because with *perfect heart* they offered willingly to the Lord" (verse 9).

Nowhere in this account is there a suggestion of "family goals" or some form of pressure. The motivating factor was a love for God and a desire to consecrate oneself fully to the service of the Lord.

The dinner: The "fellowship dinner" has been given authenticity by quoting the verse "And they did eat and drink before the Lord on that day with great gladness" (verse 22). But one should contrast the spirit of the people of David's time with that of the Israelites at the time of the building of the tabernacle in the wilderness:

> The plan of Moses to raise means for the building of the tabernacle was highly successful. No urging was necessary. Nor did he employ any of the devices to

which churches in our day so often resort. *He made no grand feast."—Patriarchs and Prophets*, p. 529. (Italics supplied.)

Obviously there was a vast difference in the attitudes of these two groups. The people of Moses' time did not need even the testimony of Moses as to what he was going to do to spur them to action. There is no record of what Moses gave to the tabernacle building fund!

Visitation pressure: There is another kind of social pressure in the traditional canvass program that many fail to understand. When a member visits another member and names an amount that the church expects the individual to give, he exerts pressure no matter how adroitly he asks for the pledge.

Man-made methods always employ some persuasive force or pressure. God's plans are always based on the individual's freedom of choice. Acceptable offerings must be the result of a heart experience under the leading of the Holy Spirit.

Individual Matter

This matter of giving has not been left to the clever manipulations of man; God has given some explicit instruction regarding it:

I saw that God's people must bring to Him a freewill offering; and the responsibility should be *left wholly upon the individual, whether he will give much or little.—Testimonies*, vol. 1, pp. 237, 238. (Italics supplied.)

Of the means which is entrusted to man, God claims a certain portion—a tithe; but He leaves all free to say how much the tithe is, and whether or not they will give more than this. They are to give as they purpose in their hearts.—*Ibid.*, vol. 5, p. 149.

God says, "much or little," "whether or not." In the final analysis the decision is left to the individual, who is free to choose how much he or she will give.

The Dynamics of God's Plan

God calls for a reform far deeper than the pocketbook;

it begins with the heart.

Many ceased to deny self, and not a few withheld their tithes and offerings. God in His providence called for a reform in His sacred work, which should *begin at the heart* and work outwardly.—*Selected Messages*, book 2, pp. 177, 178. (Italics supplied.)

No undue external pressures of any kind that appeal to the carnal nature must be used to influence people to give, for this is the test that God uses to determine their fitness for heavenly citizenship.

I saw that the cause of God is not to be carried forward by pressed offerings. God does not accept such offerings. The matter is to be *left wholly to the people*. They are not to bring a yearly gift merely, but should also freely present a weekly and monthly offering before the Lord. This work is left to the people, for it is to be to them a weekly, monthly test.—*Testimonies*, vol. 1, p. 237. (Italics supplied.)

God tests us here, by committing to us temporal possessions, that our use of these may show whether we can be entrusted with eternal riches.—*Counsels on Stewardship*, p. 22.

Much depends on *whom* we listen to. "Suggested Giving Guides" are exactly what their name implies—suggestions. The church does have an important role in communicating information, explaining needs, and suggesting how those needs may be met. But in the final analysis a person is to listen to the voice of God—not to that of man. It isn't so important what a person thinks, but it is vitally important what God thinks. Notice carefully whose voice should be heard:

The followers of Christ should not wait for thrilling missionary appeals to arouse them to action. If spiritually awake, *they would hear* in the income of every week, whether much or little, the voice of God and of conscience with authority demanding the tithes and offerings due the Lord.—*Testimonies*, vol. 4, p. 474.

One church leader, a businessman, came to me one evening during a series on stewardship education and asked, "How much do you think I ought to give?"

"I haven't the faintest idea," I replied.

"But I thought you were an expert," he countered.

"Not really," I answered, "but I know two people who do know."

"Who are they?" he inquired.

"You and God," was my reply.

He smiled and said, "You really mean that, don't you?"

"Of course I do," I said. "If I were going to invest some of my partner's money, I'd surely ask him about it."

A few nights later, just before the evening meeting was to begin, he drew me to one side and told me in confidence that he had made a decision to give a certain sum to the Lord's work. I was frankly amazed at the size of his gift.

"That must have been some conversation," I remarked.

"It was," he replied. "The other night when I went home I got down on my knees and said, 'Lord, have I been selfish?' And He said, 'You sure have!'" Then a very serious look crossed his face and he added, "You know, I love the Lord. I don't want to be selfish—and I'm going to do something about it."

How much people need to listen to God. But when they are subjected to emotional appeals, competitive approaches, or social and financial manipulations, it is next to impossible to hear God's voice at all. In reality good, well-meaning people "jam" God's communication system! The results are that people fail to listen to God's voice and become accustomed to listening to the voices of other people. This may lure them into a sense of self-satisfaction, like that of the doctor who stated:

"Whenever my church had a fund-raising campaign, I used to ask only one question, 'How much have you got me down for?' I always gave the suggested amount. But when I asked a stewardship secretary, he said he didn't know—that I should ask God. Now I am giving twice as much as I used to, and I'm increasing my giving all the time to keep up with God's blessings."

The fact that new churches and schools have been built as a result of these programs is no proof of their merit, because there have been vast systems of churches and schools that have been built through compulsion. If the end justifies the means, one might add to this list those that were constructed from funds secured by lotteries. Can gambling be justified as a means for securing funds to build God's house?! Can the bingo games, the raffles, and other questionable forms of fund raising be condoned just because they are covered with a religious garment and the funds are used for church support?

How About the Member Who Didn't Give?

Frequently a person is encountered who "didn't go along" with the program. Some have left the church—others have withdrawn into a shell of bitterness. What about these? Some have stopped giving entirely. When they do come to the realization that they have cheated not only God but themselves, they suffer pangs of remorse that the years cannot wash away. Are these to be ignored? Any plan that might drive even one person from the church is not God's plan. Jesus said, "Come unto me." He even provided room for the tares to grow with the wheat!

The only plan God ordained leaves the matter to each individual whether he will give "much or little," "whether or not." The choice must be his.

One Plan

There is no other plan for financing God's church than the one originally ordained. A faithful return of the tithe and the giving of freewill offerings will amply sustain it in every department. Every other method is a substitute, and we can make no greater mistake than to set aside God's plans for those of our own invention.